Bam
boo
zled

BAMBOOZLED
An Incarcerated Boxer Goes Undercover for
John McCain's Boxing Bill

Joe Biel

Edited by Lauren Hage, Erik Spellmeyer, and Tim Wheeler

ISBN 9781621065852

First Published May 1, 2013
First printing of 3,000 copies

Published by:

Microcosm Publishing
636 SE 11th Ave.
Portland, OR 97214
www.microcosmpublishing.com

Distributed by Independent Publisher's Group, Chicago and
Turnaround, UK

Printed in the U.S.

The primary sources for this material are the hundreds of letters from
Joey Torrey and his memoir: *Bamboozled: The Joey Torrey
Story*, which is also available from Microcosm Publishing:

Hiding out from the authorities in Mexico

Getting in the limo to go to his pro fight

Running his sports memorabilia operation from prison

Making "friends" on the outside

Contents

"As I enter my 35th year of incarceration after being eligible for parole since 1994, if there had been any lingering shreds of innocence left in me, they were dashed away within the pitiful drama of a blind judicial system and a corrupt United States Attorney General's Office.

As I feel my soul has been eaten away a little each day, each month, each year. Steadily ignored year after year as the false hopes of freedom saps my heart and breaks my spirit. Many in the world's media have claimed that my actions were grotesque consequences of well-earned despair, a metaphor for the hopelessness that I wake to with every false hope of freedom by nihilistic attorneys who hold my freedom in one hand; in exchange for a bag of silver in the other.

NO MAN'S FREEDOM SHOULD HAVE A PRICE!"

—Joey Torrey, Fall of 2012

(PREFACE)

Fear of God is what Kim Joseph Torrey, burly and heavily tattooed, might instill in a passer-by on the sidewalk. Yet Chris Baca, President/ CEO of Youth Development, Inc (YDI), a New Mexico based organization that provides assistance to youths and their families, says the former boxer and convicted murderer he often had as a guest in his home is anything but a thug. "Once you get past the exterior, this is an amazing man," he says. "Talented, intelligent, with a thirst for life."

While serving time at the Central New Mexico Correctional Facility in Los Lunas, Torrey called Baca and told him he could deliver NFL rushing leader Emmitt Smith for a paid-admission speaking engagement to benefit YDI.

"I thought, 'Yeah, and Joey could get [actor who died of AIDS] Rock Hudson to rise from the grave,'" Baca recalls. "But lo and behold, he did what he said he'd do."

Torrey's determination and ability to achieve what he sets his mind to is great, but how he ended up locked up in New Mexico is another story.

Convicted on a plea bargain in 1979 of murdering José Ramirez, a gas station attendant he claims was his boxing manager, Torrey has been in prison for two-thirds of his life.

Joey Torrey, or "Torres" as he often refers to himself, is a peculiar case. On the surface his story appears to be about justice gone awry. Aside from the particulars of an admittedly far-from-perfect criminal justice system, Joey's case asks the heavier questions. How much does one's moral compass correct itself over twenty or thirty years? What if that person—like Torrey—seems to lack solid morals in his upbringing, environment, peers, and professional life? Will decades in prison typically instill a moral compass or reduce you to the lowest common denomenator of your peers? How is it ultimately decided whether or not a person can re-integrate into "civilized" society?

The fable within this fable as well as Torrey's contradictions, inconsistencies, and idiosyncrasies make the story ever more complicated and compelling.

One thing Joey frequently sets his mind to is telling a good story. According to Joey's former probation officer, Torrey is so good at manipulation that his parents described him as a "skillful fabricator of stories who can weave fantasy and fiction together in a most convincing fashion."

Did they mean "fact" and "fiction?" Or do they mean that the fabric of his stories contain little relationship to reality— that he is so good at crafting stories and convincing himself that they are reality; that it becomes his truth? We may never know if that was a simple typo or a case of unknowingly-telling literary license.

For many years Joey told his story to celebrities and pro sports heroes who rushed to his defense and did favors for him, but they each seem to disappear from his life in a way that gives me pause. Their extreme persistence, strong words, and determination seem to suddenly disappear. Joey had a similar knack for attracting reporters to visit him in prison and prompting stories clearly written from the bond formed between them.

And perhaps the best example is my own. In 2006 I started to receive frequent and heartfelt letters at an increasingly prolific rate from Torrey in prison. He tried very hard to bond with me. He has sent me holiday cards for the past six years. He crafted beautiful portraits of my partner and I. Then he would talk about those gifts as an obligation I had to him. He was quickly able to understand my motivations and concerns in the world. What he seemed to lack in empathy he made up for in spates of apparent honesty and his ability to lick wounds and move on to the next thing he wanted from me. On some level, this is survival in prison and it is necessary to create a bond with the outside world, but Torrey takes this act to a refined art form repeatedly throughout his life. Joey's storytelling caused his "friends" from the world of professional sports to advocate his release, pay his bills, and buy him cars before they disappeared from his life.

But a few details in his story don't quite match the official one. Joey insists that the case against him is for the murder of José Ramirez but Los Angeles prosecutor Pamela Frohreich dug through a shallow grave of paperwork to discover Torrey was actually charged with murdering a 21-year-old gas station attendant named Armando Cardenas Jasso who had no connection to boxing.

Was this a paperwork error or has Joey successfully re-written his own history in his head? Since so many reporters mimicked Joey's version of events, why wasn't this discovered sooner?

Another convicted murderer who declares his own innocence after spending eighteen years in prison, Damian Echols, expresses the importance of focusing on what you have in your life. He says, rather than focusing on what you don't have, like freedom, appreciate and develop the relationships you have. Echols claims it is what guided and calmed him through his eighteen years behind bars. This is a lesson that Torrey seems to understand as frequently as he twists it.

But Joey does seem to understand the importance of having an outward appearance that he has achieved zen with his life in prison. Understandably, he does sometimes slip and complains, "Doing life for a Y.A. plea bargain? It makes you mad. It makes you really mad." In a recent letter to me, while explaining why I should send him $10,000 to hire a new attorney to appeal his case, he wrote "I don't expect you to understand, since you can walk outside and see the sunshine whenever you wish." A fair point.

By 1990 Torres had married a woman he corresponded with from New Mexico. He arranged to transfer into the New Mexico penal system.

There, he came across *coram nobis*—a procedure intended to bring factual errors or omissions to the court's attention. The former amateur boxer continued a decades long fight for his freedom. In 1998, he arranged to be transferred from New Mexico back to California.

"I needed access to California law," he says.

Torrey had appealed before and his contention remained the same. In 1980, neither the court nor his attorneys had outlined the consequences if he received expulsion from the California Youth Authority (now the Division of Juvenile Justice), and it had resulted in a sentence of life in prison.

When his new court date arrived, Thomas I. McKnew Jr, a Los Angeles Superior Court judge, vacated both Torres's guilty plea and the judgment against him.

With that, Torrey was released into a world he barely recognized.

"People asked me what my cell number is," he jokes. "I say, cell block six, cell 13. They say 'No, no, no... Your cell phone.'"

But Torrey's new-found freedom was in jeopardy from the start.

Torrey's petition of *coram nobis*, the state argued on appeal, was handled improperly—the issue was settled long ago. On May 19, 2003, Torrey stood in a Los Angeles courtroom and was ordered back to prison, and he's spent most of his time since attempting new appeals from the California prison system.

"I'm still shell-shocked," he says.

Torrey's former attorney, Verna Wefald, petitioned for a review of the decision to grant the state's appeal that had little hope for success. She had greater hope, however, for a *habeas corpus* petition she filed regarding matters far closer to the heart of the case against Torrey.

First: The only witness against Torrey, in 1978, had a prior criminal record and received immunity for his testimony.

Prosecutors did not reveal this in court.

Second: There was no eyewitness to the murder, nor was a murder weapon found.

Third: Torres was never allowed to speak on his own behalf during his original trial.

Wefald says California almost never grants parole in first-degree murder cases. Think life, she says—not 25 years.

"I've kind of lost faith in God. I really have." says Torrey.

Joey tends to follow statements like these with proclamations about how he would rather focus on the days until his next opportunity for appeal—and what he has done with his days and those remaining is what is truly important.

For a repeatedly condemned man, Torres can still muster an upbeat demeanor. He laughs, cracks jokes, and in 2003, was working the phones for YDI and doing business for Top Rank, a boxing management company.

"I did all right, huh?" he asks, then answers his own question.

"I did all right. I did all right."

Joey Torrey, 1978

Luigi, Marci, Ana, Mr. Gallo, and Bruce Trampler

A full moon shines above the glare of brilliant lights, which fade into the darkness beyond the walls and fences. Guards maintain their vigil behind protective glass in this maximum security prison. In 1998, Kim Joseph Torrey, prisoner number C-47554, serving a life sentence for murder, was placed in Corcoran.

He maintains hope for his release, which is made visually evident by his extensive collection of law books, legal pads, and manila folders and his prolific letter writing campaigns.

Joey Torrey frequently has dreams that the state comes around to serve justice as he sees it—by releasing him. He's had that dream for over twenty years. Waking up each day, reluctuant to face his reality, he begins his excercise routine. Joey knows that some of his decisions have caused others to want to kill him before that parole day ever comes.

Prisoners usually get "whacked" in the morning when they're groggy or just released from "the hole." Sometimes all a person can do is keep their mind and body in tip-top shape in case the moment to defend themself arises.

At breakfast time, Torrey might see Charlie Manson and Sirhan Sirhan, whom both share his cell block. Skilled at attaching himself to famous people, Joey claims to have known both men since he was a kid and to answer Charlie's mail, since Manson claims he can't read or write.

•   •   •

Joey was born May 4th, 1960, to a Puerto Rican father and a Sicilian mother in Brooklyn, New York. Joey says he was told that his father was offered a job in California, and moved the family there to start over, but as he grew older, he says a different story emerged. In the 1940s, a Sicilian girl wouldn't speak to a Puerto Rican man, let alone marry one. His mother's six brothers instructed his father to disappear. So Joey's father changed the family name from Torres to Torrey, a change that haunts him to this day.

As a 5'5", 140-lb kid resembling a dorky character from *Mad* magazine, Joey was and still is often accused of being a white man trying to be Latino. To make identity matters worse, his father was a VP for an ambulance company and they lived in a suburban three-bedroom ranch, vacationed in Europe, and attended church regularly.

And that confused racial heritage and search for authenticity plagued him worst in his teenage years. He grew up in what was then a more working class Panorama City. He started to get in fights with Mexican kids who thought he was white. He says he would frequently fight with his dad about changing their name. Joey idealized gang and street life and seemed bored by the suburban trappings of his youth.

At 15 years old he stole money from his parents and moved out, preferring a life of being homeless on the streets of South Central Los Angeles. Gang territory in Los Angeles was a complex issue in the 1970s and straying into someone's territory frequently caused fights. One day Joey rode the bus from the west side to the east side of LA Stopping downtown, another kid on the bus asked him the question that framed his teenaged fate: "Where you from?"

Joey says he tried to step off the bus, but the kid grabbed his arm, and they fought for what felt like hours. Eventually Joey says he grabbed the kid's throat and groin and banged him into a trash can until he passed out. The kid, "Lil Boxer," a big boxer from 18th St., became Joey's best friend and started calling Joey "Boxer." Joey claims he was accepted into the west side 18th Street gang—one of the few gangs at the time where Puerto Ricans, Cubans, and misfits congregated because Mexican gangs wouldn't take them.

His probation officer later wrote, "No one ever knew whether to take this claim seriously. It was highly unlikely an LA gang would even speak to a middle-class Caucasian youth from the San Fernando Valley."

Joey recalls going to Venice Beach with Lil' Boxer. A car drove up and a fight broke out. The police showed up and the boxers took off running, but when Joey saw Lil' Boxer get caught, he says he went back so they could go to jail together.

At the beach patrol holding facility, Joey says a police officer gave them the choice between joining the police boxing program at the 77th police station or going to juvenile hall. They both decided then and there to "Box!"

Joey wanted to spend the remainder of the night partying, so the boxers headed through the gauntlet of gang territory towards the 77th police station. That summer, Joey says the police program taught them the science of boxing.

Joey's dad once took him and Lil' Boxer to the gym for a match in East LA With Joey's dad in their corner, Lil' Boxer won the first fight, but Joey had the flu. Still, he fought. As his opponent put his gloves up for the first round, Joey's left hook ended the match as fast as it had started. Joey says his dad was frozen, mouth open in amazement.

That night, Joey's dad dropped them off on Main St., where they ate chicken wings as they strutted down skid row. They spent the night with a woman named Shondra, who had a few kids and treated them well. As a fifteen year old, Joey developed a love of gambling, cocaine, parties, and women.

In the summer of 1975, Joey was getting released from East Lake Juvenile Hall for being a runaway. Lil' Boxer picked him up, pretending to be his dad. Joey claims Shondra worked as a counselor at the very same Juvenile Hall so they drank 40 ounces around the corner and waited for her to get off work.

A 1947 Chevy pulled into the adjacent parking lot and Lil' Boxer slapped Joey, saying it was Bobby Chacon, an undefeated fighter in LA, getting ready for a shot at the title.

Through a window, Joey watched Bobby Chacon practice with Benny Urquidez at the nearby gym. To him, their motions looked like a primitive dance. He walked into the gym, and Benny's charm caught him off guard. Benny greeted Joey with a smile and introduced himself—walking him into the matted area where Bobby was hitting the heavy bag, resounding in a sharp and crisp, pop, pop, pop. Maybe it was the Colt 45 in his bloodstream or just his innate stubbornness, but for whatever reason, Joey informed Benny "The Jet" Urquidez that a good boxer would "kick the shit out of any Karate man."

Former Welterweight Champion and International Boxing Hall of Famer Carlos Palomino describes Joey at this point in his life as a "wide-eyed, happy-go-lucky kid with a lot of confidence who thought he could be a world champion."

Bobby stopped hitting the bag and turned to Benny in an awkward silence, before they started to laugh. A pissed off Joey explained, "Fool, I'm Boxer from 18th St. and just won the junior Golden Gloves. My record is 7-0, with six knockouts!" Benny, never losing his cool, explained he only fought for money and, when Joey grew up, he could bring some money in and they could tie 'em on.

They returned to working out, leaving Joey to feel like a fool before he realized he was late picking up Shondra. Joey found her standing at the corner down the street, smiling, and not even upset. Joey couldn't pick her up in front of her work because as a 30 year old social worker she could not be seen having romantic entanglements with a 15 year old street kid. Shondra held Joey's hand on the drive home as she tenderly told him that he was going to be a father.

•   •   •

Not being aware that Benny earned his living in the Orient, enjoying the undefeated title of full contact Karate champion, neither Joey nor the U.S. had developed a full appreciation of his fighting style. Joey felt that even if he could not beat Urquidez, he would learn from the experience.

That evening, Joey says he went out, stealing the stereo out of every car he found, borrowed $100 from Shondra, and walked into the Jet Center the next day with a bag full of stereos. He dropped it at the feet of Benny in the office, who was on the phone. Benny peeked in the bag, smiled, and pulled a cash roll from his pocket, "Let's do this thing."

The dojo's radio was blasting Marvin Gaye as Benny bowed and they touched gloves. As Joey began to box, he found Benny behind him. As he turned, Benny swept his front foot, sending him flying. As Joey caught air, Benny hit him with a spinning back kick to the chin. Joey says he remembers hearing the bones break as his jaw dropped. Joey woke up in the hospital with his jaw wired shut; Benny was sitting across from him. Joey wrote on his medical chart, "How did I go down? Did I go down with style? P.S: You have a light bulb out on the ceiling fixture!" Benny and Bobby couldn't stop laughing.

For the next three years, the Urquidez brothers and Bobby Chacon played a big role in Joey's life; molding him to think and behave more like a pro fighter, but Joey remained arrogant and had a hard time with defeat. Joey began to use his cocaine habit as a way to diffuse the pain while fighting.

While Shondra's belly got bigger, Joey trained at the dojo. He claims he trained with fighters that would later become legends: Superfoot Bill Wallace, Ed Parker, and Chuck Norris. By the summer of 1976, Joey began teaching a beginners class for kids 7-14. He toured the country with Benny's "LA Stars."

The Urquidez brothers were innovative in their incorporation of boxing from the waist up and Kempo from the waist down. The dance it created was known as *Akata*. This combination put their strategy decades ahead of other fighters, and it left them undefeated.

Later that year, Benny and his family created "full contact Karate to the knockout" after getting disqualified from tournaments for hitting too hard. A 16-year-old Joey helped with the first full contact Karate match.

Benny's sister, Lilly, made history by going to Japan and becoming the first woman to be given a belt as the world's full contact women's champ.

Joey claims that when he entered a disco with Manny Urquidez that the band would introduce them between songs, informing the crowd of their next fight.

One night, after a day of working out, Boxer came by the dojo as Joey and Manny were getting ready for a weekend. They planned to go to Sunset and invited Boxer along for drinks and ended up eating burritos in East LA at Manuel's. They were greeted with the three fated words that precede trouble, "Where you from?"

Joey says he tried to explain that they had fights coming up and did not want any problems. The men asked again, "Where you from?" as they stepped closer. Joey claims that Boxer said, "Fuck this shit," and pulled out a gun—shooting them both dead. Manny jumped in his car, and Joey ran to LA General Hospital, sitting in the bathroom; waiting. He called Benny, and as Joey stepped into Benny's car, Benny said, "I don't want to know shit." Boxer was charged with first degree murder. Joey did not see him again for 20 years, but wrote him often.

2

Joey started making good money in 1976, fighting full contact and teaching doctors and lawyers how to protect themselves, plus working in his brother Luigi's pizza shop. He claims to also have been running numbers for the bar next door.

One day Joey received a call from his mother, who ordered him to bring his daughter by the house. Joey hadn't seen his parents the previous year, but as he sat in the yard with his father, watching a young Sugar Ray Leonard on *Wide World of Sports*, his father bouncing Vida on his knee, his mother came outside, saying Joey had a phone call.

It was from an official of the Amateur Athletic Union (AAU). Joey looked at his father and went inside to tell Mr. Tony Cerda, chairman of the boxing department, that he weighed 146 pounds. Cerda asked, "Want to fight for the nationals this coming weekend in Anaheim?" But Joey's father, sitting next to him, told Cerda that Joey was still a juvenile.

His father went back outside. Opening another beer and slowly shaking his head, his father tried to tell Joey that the fight was a setup. "They want you to fight for the nationals on television for a spot on the 1980 Olympic team?" It dawned on Joey that his father might think that he was not good enough. "They will use you and then toss you away." Joey demanded his mother bring the baby outside and they left as his father called after them, "Run! That's all you do." Joey smiled and walked away, proclaiming. "At least I try and did not sell out my race and even my name!" Joey did not see his father again for 20 years.

•   •   •

After hanging up the phone, Benny came to the mat where Joey was shadow boxing. He inspected the scar over Joey's eye from receiving a head butt. Joey told Benny that Cerda called and asked if he could take the fight. Benny called his wife, Sara, and told her, *Call the students and their parents. They have a road trip next week for Joey's fight.*

Preferring to shadow box and move side to side, rather than train, Joey listened to music and visualized the fight in his mind. Benny told him, "Turn around and look at those people that believe in you." It was one of Benny's classic inspirational moments. Benny had told Joey that during the winter nationals he had tried to find fighters to beat Joey. "You need to be taken down a peg or two...The problem is, you beat them all!" According to Joey, Benny expected him to win the Olympics in a couple years and turn pro.

Benny's own popularity was soaring at the time. So when they arrived at the event center, Benny kept everyone at arms length, to be professional. They headed to the dressing room where it was a different scene than Joey was used to—kids dressed in silk robes with their names stitched on the back. Benny informed Joey that he was fighting Tony Cerda Jr., the event director's son, a southpaw fighter (leads with his right hand), who hits hard. The fight appeared to be designed for the son to make the Nationals and a spot on the 1980 Olympic team.

The referee came to Joey's corner, checked his mouth piece and cup, and directed him to the middle of the ring. He then stated, "In the red corner, fighting out of Pomona, California, the two-time Golden Glove Champ, three time AAU Champ, and heading for the 1980 Olympic team—Tony Cerda, Jr. In the blue corner, fighting out of the Urquidez Brother's Gym, in Los Angeles, California Junior Golden Glove Champ—Joey Torres." Returning to the corner, Benny stuck in Joey's mouthpiece and slapped him. Joey looked up, slapped his gloves, and heard, "Seconds out. Ding, ding!"

Tony stepped back and got up on his toes, hitting with five punches that Joey did not block or return. For the first round, he tattooed with lefts and rights that had Joey's head snapping back, and then to the left with rushing hooks. Joey claims they did not hurt and the kid had a weak punch. In reality, it was probably the effects of the cocaine. In the second round, Joey says he felt the flow, got up on his toes, and pounded his gloves together. Cerda hit Joey's face with his right glove. Then Joey slid under the returned right, slipped to the left, and caught Cerda's liver and kidney with a hook as he felt the wind go out of him. Joey stood up to throw his right, but Cerda was not there; his arms were around Joey's waist as he slid to the canvas, and the referee entered on seven, eight, nine. Benny lifted Joey's arms as the bell tolled and Joey heard "...and the new, Amateur Athletic Union Welterweight Champion—Joey Torres."

Joey says he looked into the audience and saw Tony Cerda Senior in shock. The caravan of students and friends were going crazy, rubbing it in on the locals. They went out to Denny's and then Joey and Manny took off to party.

•　　•　　•

At 15 years old, Joey admits his ego was out of control. He felt he could do no wrong and had no one to answer to. He would later speak to Mike Tyson about this, who pointed to himself and said, smiling, "That's why I'm broke." As an amateur, Joey was not allowed to make money from boxing or accept money from sponsors.

Joey spent the end of 1976 in Stockton, California, training with the light-heavyweight Alvaro Yaqui Lopez, who invited him to take his game to another level by training with Thai kickboxers. After Joey won the regionals and was making strides for the Nationals, the managers were on him as he entered the Jet Center, knowing he'd be big money once he won a major. With so few people looking out for the best interest of young fighers, it's no wonder that so many develop big egos and get into serious trouble.

Joey was fighting with the LA Stars, traveling, waking up in hotel rooms, not knowing what city he was in.

Joey claims that while he watched Bobby Chacon getting his title shot, he noticed a kid about his age sit next to him. The smiling kid supposedly extended his hand and said in broken English that he was a fan of Joey's, and his name was José Ramirez-Cardenas de Mexico.

Joey says Ramirez claimed to be a manager and named fighters that Joey had never heard of. Ramirez saw Carlos and reached over to shake his hand, but Carlos ignored him. Ramirez supposedly went back to watching the fight and expressing an interest in managing Joey.

According to Joey, their arrangement was that after the Olympics, they could turn professional, and Ramirez would pay Joey's living expenses until they "made" it. Carlos Palomino, years later, describes the situation as "When [you're a kid and] someone says to you, 'Stick with me, I'll make you a world champion,' you tend to believe that."

Joey says Ramirez offered him fights in Mexico and "tough man" fights, and that they could keep it a secret. Joey says that as Ramirez got up to leave, he was handed a business card and some fifty dollar bills that "smiled up at him."

Joey began to add cocaine to his nasal spray to numb the pain of the blows. With this formula, he was a fairly unstoppable warrior, but it didn't stop after his fights. As a sixteen year old, he began going out to clubs and doing coke at all hours and not sleeping for days.

At this point in a boxer's career—where they are a serious amateur—all of their time must go into training to compete and move up into the professional world, but without any way to pay their living. They are stuck in a moral and financial impasse. They can either be wealthy to begin with or are forced to find a way to make a living in addition to forty hours of training each week. Joey told his friend that he made a living as a boxer but investigators revealed that he worked at his brother's pizza shop. If he had other sources of income, as he claims, it's unclear.

In the spring of 1977 Shondra and their daughter Vida moved back to Santo Domingo without Joey, and he never heard from either one again, but Joey met a new girl in the doctor's office while getting a B-12 shot. Her name was Dolly, and her family liked him. Her dad loved fighting, so Joey invited him to his next event in San Diego.

His opponent was very tall, so as Benny yelled, "body!" Joey took to his opponents' body with punches and kicks until he was crumpled on the floor and the referee raised Joey's hand. At that time his record was 18-0, with 14 KO's in full contact Karate, and 48-14 with 28 KO's in the AAU.

Joey claims that Ramirez approached him after the fight and handed him a card for the Beverly Hills Hotel, saying "Party tonight."

Later that week, Benny pulled Joey aside and informed him that it was time to get his own place to live. Joey moved into the Cecil Hotel on Main St. in downtown LA. His routine included buying a bowl of rice from Johnny's shrimp boat, across the street from the world famous Main Street Gym, where managers would buy and trade boxers. By noon, Joey had his hands taped and would be hearing out managers in the gym. They started noticing Joey after he won the AAU fight the previous year. They offered cars, apartments, and money.

Joey focused on sparring with professional champs while they were getting ready for their title defenses. Fighters from around the world came to the Main Street Gym in the 70s: Duran, Mardrano, Arguello, Ali, and Lopez.

Joey claims Ramirez had paid his rent for a couple months at the Cecil, so he had the time to be present on 18th St. for all "street activities" or as he puts it, to "be gangster."

While Joey was suited to life in the ring, most of his problems occurred outside of it. One day, on his way to visit his mom, who had offered a surprise, Joey sat on the back of the bus. He says he was wearing his blue AAU jacket with his name and record stitched on the front, daydreaming of how far he'd come and thinking he had a chance of being on the 1980 Olympic team.

He says he awoke to three men getting on the bus loudly at the Vine stop. It was typical of every thug in LA to walk to the back of the bus and that's where this trio was headed when they locked eyes on him. The lead guy was almost on him as one of them was throwing fists in the air and pointing to him, demanding, "Where you from?"

In one second, Joey had to punk out and say, "Nowhere," or claim his residence and gang, but declining a fight wasn't how Joey was wired. As soon as he claimed his territory, one of the men grabbed the chrome balance bars on the bus and leapt in the air, kicking Joey in the side of the head with such force that his head shattered through the window.

Joey says he started to pass out but managed to reach for the buck knife in his belt while ducking the next kick, then planted the blade deep into his attacker's stomach. Joey stepped over the body, advancing towards his buddies, as they appeared to contemplate whether to fight or run. Joey jumped off the bus on Vine and was arrested a few blocks away.

Joey sat in the police station while the cops waited to see if the stab victim would survive or not.

·   ·   ·

That evening, after providing a fake name and age to the cops, the call came that the guy would live and Joey would be charged with attempted murder for lacerating his liver. Bail was set and Joey says Ramirez sent his sister to bail him out. Later that week, Joey was arrested at the gym when someone told the cops his real name and identity as a minor. He spent the next few months in juvenile hall and says he thought about Shondra and Vida. Seventeen years old and living fast, Joey made a deal and was sentenced to 18 months in Camp Glenn Rocky, north of LA, where he had been sent before as a runaway.

In a few weeks he had adjusted to his new surroundings. Joey ran in the morning and lifted weights in the evening. His mother visited with Dolly and her daughter Blanca, but then he remembered he had never learned what his mother's surprise was. Bouncing Blanca on his knee, Joey's mother rubbed Dolly's belly and told him, "You're gonna be a daddy, Son." Joey looked at Dolly, who smiled and shook her head up and down. His mother grabbed Blanca and gave them an hour alone. Afterward, they laughed, and began writing everyday. She visited every weekend.

In hindsight, Joey claims he grew up a lot during that winter of 1977. Dolly had gotten in contact with his other daughter and made him sell his car and send her money. Joey remained in good shape, excited to return to the ring. He planned to be released to Dolly, as she was an adult.

But first Joey was called to the warden's office for a special visit. Walking into the office, he saw his mom sitting, eyes swollen from crying. Dolly's father stepped between them to hug Joey. He told Joey, crying, that Dolly and Blanca were gone. They had been electrocuted in the bathtub by short-circuited christmas lights.

•　　•　　•

Joey was released early on a rainy January morning in 1978. He visited the graves of Dolly, Blanca, and his unborn. While Joey developed a lot of frustration towards the people in his life, he had lacked the requisite amount of time to have a falling out with Dolly, so he continues to remember her well.

Joey began gaining weight and eventually expanded out of his weight class, losing his chance of going to the Olympics. He cites the loss of his loved ones as the reason, but admits he continued to use cocaine in the youth authority.

Benny told him that there was something big coming in a few months and he was leaving for Japan to finalize the deal. Japanese fighters were challenging the LA Stars and America's best to a full contact, no holds barred fight and invited Joey. This was to be his second to last fight and losing seven pounds, the newly-147-pound Joey agreed.

In the meantime, Joey says Ramirez asked him to drive into Lancaster to recruit some youngsters for the Golden Gloves tournament. Joey says Ramirez was pissed off the entire drive—talking about how Joey screwed him over by screwing up his body. Joe claims Ramirez had setup deals that he had been counting on Joey for. Joey said they could still arrange some fights in Mexico, explaining that he was going to be 18 in a few months and wanted a major full contact fight.

At the venue in Lancaster, Joey says he was cornered by the local TV crew, asking why he was not in the Nationals and if he quit boxing. Out of the corner of his eye, Joey saw his brother Luigi talking to a biker and pointing at him as Ramirez is laughing, counting bills, and handing them to the bartender. From the background, Luigi is giving Joey the left, right, signal. Then the biker was on top of him and Joey says he gave him numerous uppercuts while the biker tried to headbutt him. As the biker went on one knee, Joey says he grabbed the man's hair and put a knee to his nose, wondering if they'd add this fight to his record.

•　　•　　•

Joey says that Luigi was 5'4", 300 lbs, with a cigar forever planted in his mouth that was bigger than his head. His style was straight out of a 40s gangster movie. In public school, Joey says he was visited by the FBI and shown pictures of his brother Luigi with Jimmy Ratianno, Frank Sica, Bill Bonnano, and Mr. Gambino.

Joey says that one day in the pizza shop, the phone rang. His brother made a face; which normally meant that it was someone important and to be quiet. He answered in Sicilian, tore off the apron, and turned to Joey, "You wanna go for a drive?"

In "the family" there were allegedly two bosses. Frank Sica was from the valley and rumor reported that he ran everything from prostitution to numbers. The big boss supposedly was Jimmy the Weasel and his sidekick, Ray Giarusso, whose operation was located in Hayward, California.

Joey got in the car with his brother and they drove in silence. Luigi was holding the wheel with such force that his knuckles were white. Joey had never seen him like this. They arrived at a gated compound where Joey says Luigi was identified as a friend. Joey says he walked into a room of cigar smoke and old timers smelling like Hai Karate Cologne. He says he recognized Fratianno, who he describes looking like a mouse. Joey says "Uncle" Frank Sica asked him to throw a hook, and the old timers tried to show him the proper way. Uncle Frank gave him a hug and said, "Thanks." Joey says he wondered why. As they left, he was smacked, kissed, and cheek-pinched all the way out the front door.

On the trip back, he says his brother seemed happier than ever. At the split in the Grapevine, instead of going left, Luigi veered into the Los Angeles lane. Joey remembers Luigi telling him, "It's your time to grow up and become a man," and "if you're gonna dance in life, you gotta pay the band." As they drove into the Hollywood area, Joey says Lugi informed him that "some piece of shit" had ripped off Uncle Frank and the family for six figures and needed to be "baptized."

The man, supposedly, was the owner of Steve's Mufflers in North Hollywood, and Joey says as Luigi was telling him about Steve, he reached under his seat and handed Joey a leather slackjack and instructed him to whack Steve a couple times in the head. "Do not kill him! Make sure he gets the hint and pays his bill."

Joey says he felt that being in Vietnam had taken away his brother's conscience and that, without a second thought, if the family told his brother to put a bullet in him, that Luigi would make him dig his own grave.

Joey says they stayed at a hotel on Ventura Blvd. drinking wine and falling asleep to Johnny Carson. Later that night, Joey says Luigi was getting nervous as they parked in front of Steve's, telling him what to do, and sweating. Joey says Luigi calmly whispered, "You mess this up, they'll bury us both."

The mark got out of his car and unlocked the garage. Joey says he stepped inside and hit him a couple shots, instructing him to pay his bills. As Joey turned to leave, he says it felt so good that he turned around and hit Steve a few more times.

Back in Lancaster Joey says they stopped off on the highway to make a call at one of Frank's pizza places. The brothers looked up as Uncle Frank's caddie supposedly rolled into the parking lot. Joey says he strolled to the back room and palmed the .38. Joey claims that Frank walked in, all smiles, with a phony painted on tan. "I was on my way to Vegas and wanted a good pie," he reportedly said, with two goons standing behind him.

Joey says Frank gave Luigi a nod to go in the back, leaving him with two broken-nosed men as wide as the booth they sat in. Joey broke the silence, recognizing traits of "boxer's nose." The one in front also had cauliflower ear. One thug introduced himself, and Joey recognized the name as a contender in the 1940s. Joey says he took his finger off the hammer of the gun he was holding under the table; his body language relaxed. The other thug was at the jukebox, singing along to Dean Martin. Uncle Frank reportedly emerged from the back, looked down on Joey, rolled his eyes, and walked out. Luigi grabbed a bottle of wine, sat next to Joey, and supposedly poured out rolls of bills on the table from a paper bag.

Joey claims that as he was taking off the rubber bands, Luigi noticed the gun and smiled. Joey asked why Uncle Frank rolled his eyes. Luigi puffed on his giant cigar, supposedly responding, "Uncle Frank received a package this afternoon from Steve filled with more than six figures!" Joey says they were counting out the excess.

Frank wanted this guy baptized and you broke the mark's nose, ribs, and eye socket. Frank wanted a baseball bat to the knees. Joey says he crunched his shoulders and looked at Luigi, "Then why did you give me a five pound blackjack?"

Joey says he left for the gym after counting out 50 grand, marking the first time in his life with $25,000 in his pocket.

Joey loved money and could never earn this much while living with his parents and working in a pizza shop. It's almost no wonder he continued chasing the kind of money he could only get from crime.

Six weeks before the epic fight in Sacramento, Joey stopped the partying, coke, and sex. It was making his legs weak. He stopped lifting weights.

The phone rang, and it was Rueben Urquidez, Benny's older brother, who abruptly told Joey, "We have to talk. You have mail here." Joey was concerned because he was not close to Rueben, so it had to be something substantial. Joey says he took a shower, put on some Coltrane, and drove into the Valley.

Rueben opened the office door and waved Joey to sit down. Reuben looked Joey up and down and said, "I am against you fighting in Sacramento because you have no concern for anyone but yourself, and this is a big thing for our family and for martial arts. I have been informed that you're fighting Shig Fugayama, and this man is tough, to say the least." He went on to tell Joey that the judges came to a middle ground on what would be allowed in this event. The Martial Arts Federation agreed that there would be no sweeps, no groin shots; but knees were legal. Each fighter has to throw six kicks and six punches each round or be disqualified.

Joey had no problem with the rules except for no sweeps—he loved to sweep the front foot and leap in with the left hook or spinning back kick.

Joey trained with Benny, learning by watching, for five weeks. The difference in rules would make a different fight, and Joey had the option to pull out at any time. Benny instructed Joey to make sure to get the six kicks and punches out of the way and concentrate on winning. Benny slowly lifted a knee, pulling his head down and touching Joey's nose, letting Joey know that this was Fugayama's bread and butter!

Joey says he didn't talk to the media because he was running the fight through his mind and trying to visualize the outcome. As he walked into the arena from the dressing room, Joey says he had never seen so many Japanese men. Every seat was filled. Joey watched a tiny man step up on the canvas, wrapped in the rising sun flag. Joey says he approached him, smiling, trying to shake his hand with the gloves on.

The lights went out in the arena, and through the smoke-filled ring, the referee called them to the center. It was the first time Joey was taller than an opponent.

Joey says the man's face looked like it'd been hit flush with a shovel. His eyebrows were replaced by scar tissue. He had no nose, only two holes. His ears were inside-out from cauliflower syndrome. The left ear was swollen and red.

Shig approached Joey, guns blazing; left, right, and he was backed into a corner as his knee struck Joey's thigh and hips before connecting a head-butt. Frozen and locked up, Joey attempted left hooks to the jaw, but caught his elbows back in the face. The referee broke them apart. Joey was able to throw six punches and six kicks so when the bell rang, he was relieved.

Reuben was calm, and Benny said, "Get on your toes and box."

Joey came out and they touched gloves. He got on his toes; jab, jab, right, roundhouse flush on his face, but with no effect. Joey's right thudded against his opponent's face. He says he saw blood coming from Shig's ear.

Joey stayed on his toes the rest of the match to keep some distance between them. In the sixth round the referee stopped the fight to have the doctor look at Shig's closed eye and ear; which was almost severed in half. Joey wasn't doing much better with both eyes nearly shut.

By the 7th round Joey was out of gas. After training aggressive forward motion, it was exhausting to be backing up for six rounds instead. Joey had Shig in the corner and leaned down for a body shot, but Shig grabbed the back of his head, connecting his knee to Joey's face five times. Joey heard his nose crack and felt the swelling begin.

In the 8th round Joey says he caught his second wind, got up on his toes, and started hitting with left, right, left, right combinations as blood sprayed back on his face. Joey remembers returning to his corner and not being able to see. Shot and surrendering, Rueben woke him up with ice.

Through two slits, Joey says he saw the referee checking him out. He felt confident the ref would stop the fight, but instead, the ref grabbed Joey's arm and marched him to the middle of the ring, raising his hand in victory! Shig's corner had tossed in the towel. Joey felt the audience throwing things at him that hit him in the face. After Rueben stepped in to hold a towel over his head, Joey realized the crowd was throwing money. Joey says he hugged Shig as he lost his last sliver of vision.

•   •   •

Joey turned 18 and bought a 1978 Harley Sportster. Riding on Manchester Blvd. on his way to take his newest girlfriend to a baseball game, Joey claims he turned left on 43rd and saw someone punching a little girl in the face. He says there was a crowd beginning to surround them but no one was stopping it. Joey says he ran at the attacker and kicked him against a store front. Turning to check on the girl, Joey says he saw a bullet coming at him from the downed man. The first bullet tore through his thigh, throwing him back. The second bullet caught him an inch below the knee cap. The shooter took off running.

Joey says he crawled over to his bike, slid his bad leg over, and rode off to the General Hospital, as his blood boiled on the engine head. Joey woke up days later with his leg in an open cast with bullet holes and puss.

Joey thought he'd never fight again. The bullets crushed his tibia and shattered the fibula. He still wears a leg brace to this day and "walks like a duck" as he puts it. Word on the street was that Joey was shot by some guy named Red, from Grape St., Watts. Joey was released from the hospital on a Friday morning.

The cast was supposed to be on for six months before his knee would be reconstructed, but he grew impatient. Joey claims he was owed money by Ramirez for the tough guy fights and money in trust from the Steve's Muffler baptism, though it's hard to believe even a young Joey trusting his fortune to anyone when he could be spending it on prostitutes and cocaine.

Joey could walk with a cane as long as he locked his thigh, giving him control of his knee. Joey walked slowly, downstairs to the café, to the payphone and found Ramirez was in Yuma, Arizona with Joey's brother, Luigi! According to Joey, Luigi and Ramirez were business partners.

A few weeks later Joey walked into the Main St. gym with two prostitutes, Sonya and Emma, looking for Ramirez and his money. Joey needed help up the flight of one hundred stairs. Joey says he felt like damaged goods in the gym and that no one even wanted to say "hello." Carlos saw Joey's cane and walked over, shaking his head, giving him a hug. Joey informed him, "Never stop to help anyone!"

Carlos supposedly informed Joey, "Ramirez was living at the track and lost everything; going from a Benz to the bus." Carlos offered to float Joey some money, then went back to his workout.

After they left, a gang unit police car cut them off in the crosswalk and put Sonya and Emma in the back seat, on the grounds that they were prostitutes. Joey claims one cop walked him down the alley behind 4th St. and proceeded to beat him with his nightstick. He claims the officer called another car and had Joey arrested for pimping and pandering. After this incident, Joey's bad leg was a mess and his cane was broken in half.

While we don't know what Joey may have done to escalate this situation, this interaction points to an aspect of the justice system where fear and intimidation won't ever give people on the streets rehabilitation or better opportunities. Joey's own budding lucrative career of threats and intimidation was hard to trifle with. It had career perks that couldn't be replaced by working in a pizza shop.

Joey says he gave the police a phony name and called the only person he could think of to bail him out: Luigi. Luigi answered the phone and within an hour Joey was out. Meeting at the front door of the police station, Joey says Steve from the muffler shop was standing there with another roll of money for him.

Joey had a "friend," JoJo, who lived out on Venice Beach and as she rang his room, Joey grabbed his bag, hugged the girls, tossed Emma the keys to his Harley, and told her to sell it. Joey hobbled into JoJo's car and rolled away, past the Crash unit, who he says was watching his every move. Joey felt good when the hospital set his leg again, put a hot cast on, and gave him crutches. The doctor instructed him to rest, and that is what Joey had in mind as they pulled into the Central Food Market on Hill St. Joey bought bags and bags of food, spending hundreds of dollars. Feeling ever so secure with his cast, they arrived at JoJo's home on the beach as the sun was setting.

Joey still had a serious cocaine habit to pay for and kept thinking about the money he felt Ramirez owed him as he walked on the beach. Sonya and Emma visited on the weekends, walking the boardwalk with him, telling Joey stories about Main St. that were likely to make him seethe with more anger. On weekdays, JoJo and Joey were tanning on the roof when she mentioned calmly that she was five weeks pregnant. Without boxing, Joey had no income. Not one to let things go easily or be forgiven, Joey says he became increasingly determined to find Ramirez.

Joey was sitting on the boardwalk when he saw Sonya get out of a taxi. With the weight of the world on her shoulders, Sonya slumped on the bench next to Joey and handed him an envelope with Emma's handwriting on it. Joey saw a few hundred dollars as he opened it. Joey says Sonya burst into tears and said that Emma was found dead in Griffith Park with her throat slashed—victim number 6 of the Skid Row Slasher.

Joey sat on the bench looking out into the ocean. Sonya put her head on his shoulder as JoJo walked up and held her. The next day, Joey and Sonya went to the morgue and used the Harley money to bury Emma.

It was the summer of 1979. JoJo was well into her pregnancy, and Joey was playing a shell game with money to keep up. One day when he returned from his daily walk, Ramirez had called.

Joey expressed to Luigi that Ramirez, in his purview, had burned him. Joey says Luigi told him, "Do what you have to do," and kissed his cheek. Joey didn't see Sonya and JoJo, again, and didn't see his brother for another 30 years.

Joey claims he took a taxi to see Ramirez. Not needing crutches anymore due to a rubber stopper on his cast foot, Joey says he rolled up the front of Ramirez's office and saw him on the phone. Ramirez reportedly looked up and smiled, putting something into the top drawer.

Joey says he stood there waiting for Ramirez to hang up. When he finally did, Joey says he demanded all of his money. He says Ramirez peeled off five hundred and laid it in front of Joey. Joey says he demanded five grand and that Ramirez informed Joey he was washed up and he'd taken Ramirez's best girl; Emma.

Joey says Ramirez opened the drawer and pulled out a .25 automatic pistol and raised it at him. Joey claims he grabbed Ramirez's wrist, pointing the gun against Ramirez's shoulder, pulling the trigger with his other hand. Joey claims he never robbed the safe (which the transcripts seem to support) and instructed Ramirez to call 911 before taking a taxi to the airport and flew to Miami, then a Greyhound to New York City.

The facts diverge here in numerous ways from the way Joey tells it. Pamela Frohreich, the Los Angeles prosecutor investigating Joey's case dug into the meat and potatoes of his story.

"A lot of prominent people believed Joey, but nobody bothered to check the facts," said Frohreich. "That includes Joey himself, because I believe he has convinced himself of his story. He used that story to talk himself into two years of freedom."

Joey actually fled to New Orleans after the shooting but was found by the police when he returned to Los Angles two weeks later. The man he was charged with murdering seemed to have no apparent links to boxing and was 21-year-old Armando Cardenas Jasso. The gun used to kill Jasso was reportedly a .25 cal that was sold or loaned (accounts differ) to Joey under the name "Boxer" by people who claimed he was living with them at the time.

The scene of the murder is also notably different. Jasso was a lone night time gas station attendent. In a somewhat cartoonish scenario, drivers refueling at that Texaco station on Florence Avenue in Downey couldn't believe their good fortune. There was not an attendant in sight and so, on June 18, 1979, they drove off, one by one, into the night without paying for their gas.

For more confusion, Jose Ramírez is the name of a Lightweight division amateur boxer who wasn't born until 1992. It seems almost as probable that Joey would borrow this name through his routine interest in following his favorite sport.

The curious thing is that Joey's story is different in almost every fundamental detail, even ones that wouldn't point to his innocence or absolve him of the crime. In one interview he uses the passive verb, "the gun went off," as if it was merely a disassociated event unrelated to the actions of any person. For further head scratching, while robbery was listed as the motive for the murder, as Joey asserts, the police documents say that the safe was never opened. Other reports say it was opened and that Joey stole $335. So what actually took place? Was Jasso the real name of Ramirez? Has Joey merely created an elaborate fiction over the years and convinced himself of its truth?

June 25, 1979—A freshly nineteen year old Joey worried about what would become of him. He says he called an old friend who informed him that the murder was all over the T.V. and Ramirez had died, but that the police were looking for a six foot black man, so he should come back to LA.

Joey's "friend," Edward Santana, and his wife picked him up at the LA bus depot, and they changed for a party at the Paladium. "Mr. Ralph," a security guard, told Joey to get rid of his gun if he's packing because the place was surrounded and to head for the back entrance. Joey says he walked off the dance floor and opened a door to find guns drawn on him.

It turns out Santana had been brought in by the police earlier that night on an unrelated crime. He confessed to loaning Joey a .25 caliber automatic like the one used in the gas station murder. Santana told the police that Joey had confessed to the deed and even said, "I hope the fucker dies."

Joey was returned to LA County Jail, where he says he received a visit from the FBI and the task force who had just arrested Luigi in Yuma, AZ; supposedly, according to what sounds like Joey's wild imagination, driving a gas tanker full of weed and cocaine. Joey claims the FBI were tipped off by Ramirez.

Joey says the FBI brought up Uncle Frank Fratianno, 18th St., and everything people had given them to get reduced sentences. Joey claims he refused a deal and was charged with murder one, looking at the death penalty or life in prison without parole.

•　　　•　　　•

With Santana as the prosecution's only witness, the DA was nervous enough about his testimony to offer Joey a deal: five years in juvenile hall.

Joey sat alone in the LA County Jail for a year, with decisions to be made. Joey says he was not happy with his "dump truck attorney" who offered him the 3-5 years in the Youth Authority with a "promise" that Joey would be out in 18 months. In the worst case scenario, according to Joey's memory of their conversation, he could be held until he was 25 years old. The attorney informed Joey that the only evidence was Santana identifying Joey as the murderer, based on Joey's confession that he beat Ramirez up, but not with the intention of murdering him.

Joey claims an off-duty officer identified someone else that saw him at the Texaco, who, finding this odd, went to look for Ramirez. Joey claims the officer walked into the office to find the body.

Faced with the death penalty or life in prison, Joey figured "Why not plead out and go get in shape to be out in no time?" The attorney supposedly advised, "They're gonna bring out your organized crime history, your brother, Uncle Frank, and now the FBI is interested." Putting his hand on Joey's shoulder, he supposedly advised that Joey take the plea bargain.

The same day, at the sentencing hearing, the judge asked if any deals had been made in order to enter this plea of guilty. Joey stood and informed the judge that he was promised by the California Youth Authority not to exceed his 25th birthday if he entered a guilty plea. Joey claims the judge turned to the district attorney, who confirmed this oral agreement. Joey was ordered to another division to accept the plea.

Court Transcript:

Judge: Do you understand what robbery is, Mr. Torrey?
Torrey: Yes, I do.
Judge: Do you understand robbery is the taking of property from another by force or violence, and with the intent to permanently deprive that person of that property?
Torrey: Yes, I do.

Judge: Now, you also understand that if you wanted to go to trial on this case, that you have the statutory right to the process of this court to compel the attendance of all witnesses on your behalf?

Torrey: Yes, I do.

Judge: Do you give up that right?

Torrey: Yes, I do.

Judge: Do you further understand this: If you are sent to state prison, that upon release from state prison that you would be on parole for a period of up to three years?

Torrey: Yes.

Judge: You also could be sent to the California Youth Authority, in which event they could retain you there until the age of twenty five. Do you understand that?

Torrey: Yes, I do.

Judge: My further understanding is that the probation and sentence hearing will take place in Department "E" and our further understanding is that the judge in Department "E" has indicated that he will be committing the defendant to the California Youth Authority at that time. Is that correct?

Mr. Romeyn: That's the people's understanding.

Judge: Mr. Torrey, is that your understanding?

Torrey: Yeah.

*With Donna Summer singing "Bad Boy,"
the bus driver pulls into the yard at the*
Southern California reception center for the
Youth Authority, in Norwalk. As the driver turns
off the radio on a rainy February in 1980, the leg shackles
are taken off.

The California Youth Authority of the 70s and 80s was
violent, and Joey says his reputation as Boxer from 18th St. was
known to the other residents from the moment he stepped
off the bus. There's a peculiar irony: No one challenges an
Olympic swimmer to a race but every street fighter wants to
challenge a ring fighter.

When Joey was sent to YTS, a youth facility in Ontario, CA,
his reputation followed him—from the last guy he fought, to
the people whose scam he was interfering with, to the older
brother of the guy from the other side of the ring. As a fighter
on the inside, a person's worth is judged by the last ass kicked
down the totem pole—until their friends come back to give
you a beatdown. If you unknowingly brawled with a gang
member from Temple Street, years later every member in the
joint can be after you for that.

•   •   •

The week Joey turned 21 he says he recognized a face in his
cell block but couldn't place it. The man grinned at him,
menacingly.

Joey says the man approached him in the gym, training. He
claims the man called him a "no good Mexican" and he was

"gonna pay" to which Joey responded "I am Puerto Rican, and in closing: Fuck you in the neck!"

The guards were watching so the man took off as Joey went back to work on the heavy bag. When Joey asked around, he learned this was the man who had shot him from Grape St., Watts. Joey claims he knocked him out the same night he learned the man's identity.

After dinner the next night, Joey says he was warned to look out for a hit on him. A few days later he found his cell door abruptly opened. Guards ran in and handcuffed him, took him to a strip cell, hosed him off, and questioned him. The man who shot him had been hung in an apparent suicide—except with his hands tied behind his back.

Joey claims he spent his time in an empty cell with no light and one blanket, not even aware of the man's death until the investigation about it.

•　　•　　•

After that incident, Joey was transferred to northern California, to a facility called Preston Youth Facility, in Ione, where he is again imprisoned 33 years later, on the same property as the Mule Creek State Prison.

In the summer of 1981, Preston was where "troubled" inmates were sent to separate them from rival gangs. In the 1980s, the Youth Authority focused on sports at least as much as rehabilitation, and it had a boxing program. So according to Joey, he was traded by the warden at Preston to the northern facility in return for a basketball player. Joey's new home was heavily occupied by members of Mexican gangs.

After several trips to solitary confinement ("the hole"), Joey says he was put to work teaching boxing to the other inmates daily. He says they frequently embraced the contradictions of letting a rival gang carry one of their members off the floor instead of helping them up yourself.

Joey learned that he was a skilled illustrator and began creating tattoo patterns, portraits, and whatever people would commission from him, in exchange for food. His work began appearing in *Low Rider* and *Teen Angel* magazines.

Joey started to correspond with many people, re-building his connection to the outside world through the postal system. One woman who particularly caught his attention was Maria, who began visiting Joey with her son, TJ, on the weekends. Joey spent his days training in the gym, planning on making a comeback when he expected to be released in 16 months, despite statements that he was washed up and done for.

As his release date approached, Joey was issued a gate pass; meaning he could work outside of the prison grounds. He became a bus boy at the Denny's in the port of Stockton. Joey said he would go through each week trying to remember to tell Maria to buy a gun at the pawnshop, but each time she visited, Joey says he would be distracted playing with TJ, and forget to mention it. So one day Joey returned to his cell block and wrote her a letter, instructing her to buy a gun. He says his reasoning was that it would be an item for her own protection until he was around to protect her, himself.

At Denny's on Monday, while Joey was telling the waitresses about Hollywood and "the gangster life" and drinking a pint of Hennesy, he was called up front over the speaker to see the transportation cops.

Instead of the usual routine, they turned him around and put the bracelets on. Officer Rudy said they intercepted a letter saying that Joey was trying to purchase a weapon. Since all mail coming and going to the prison is read, when prosecutors reviewed the letter, it was clear to them that Joey was requesting that she obtain a gun for his use. He was caught as she tried to allegedly smuggle said gun into his lockup. He was apparently still feeling a little invincible.

Joey remembers the situation a little differently. He says that he had already told Rudy about the gun in advance but due to the Youth Authority being consolidated into the Department of Corrections in 1982, there was a need to crack down under the new management.

Joey was then transferred to Tracy Prison, which he claim was then known as "Gladiator School." As a youth inmate in a state prison, Joey was put in a single cell, while other inmates were double celled. As he was brought in, the prison was on lockdown due to an ongoing gang war.

Joey says he sent a message to one of the guys from 18th St. asking for some coffee and 411. He received some coffee, a big knife, a chess board (to put in his pants as a shield) and a note that read, "It's on! Watch your back!"

This particular prison's cast included: the Mexican Mafia, La Eme, the Aryan Brotherhood, the Black Guerilla Family, and a melting pot of Cubans, Ricans, Haitians, Native Americans, and more. Every group has a designated shot caller, who represents the group to all inmates, administration, and guards. Like a state senator, the shot caller is a lifer who has the keys to the yard.

He was still a kid, really, and thought he was going home in a few months—working at Denny's, drawing, seeing Maria... and now, facing a situation where he could expect to die in prison.

On his first Monday, Joey was guided out to the yard. Two men ran past and the 5th guy ahead of him was stabbed five times in the neck before they ran off. He died running after them. The prison stayed in lockdown for another month.

It is, at moments like these, a time to question how much rehabilitation is expected to occur in this institution, how responsibly public money is being spent, and to what end. When prisoners kill each other, it is merely held up as an opportunity to ask for more funding. Who is that helping?

Joey was scheduled for a parole board hearing in 1982 and he expected to go home, wherever that might be. Joey started working out hard and got down to 165 pounds. His knee was feeling better from the weights and his daily runs alongside the "onion field murderer" from Bakersfield. Once a week, Joey invited someone to his cell or the shower to box.

The next few weeks were the craziest. Joey was met in the big yard by a couple of La Emes who escorted him to their shot caller—"some fool from the Venice gang" that Joey had met when he lived with JoJo. The shot caller was cool and respectful to Joey but supposedly wanted 18th St. to pay La Eme. If they didn't pay, a green light would be issued, meaning that any La Eme could kill an 18th St. member without ramifications. Joey explained that he was neither Mexican nor about to pay anyone.

In the eyes of any gang from La Cosa Nostra Joey was neither white nor Mexican, but Joey's lack of racial identity was of little concern to any gang's bottom line.

A few days before his parole board hearing, Joey says he started to carry a knife, the tip pricking his knee every time he took a step. He says it made him alert and never complacent. The night before the hearing, Joey stayed up all night with his legal folder, letters of support, and new marriage certificate to Maria. Joey had no family left—Luigi was in prison, the Gambinos, Genoveses, and Bonannos were dying or snitching each other out. His relationships mostly existed in the postal system.

Knowing the parole board could release him on the spot, Joey was eager to stand out. The morning as his name was called on the loud speaker to report, many lifers wished him good luck.

When Joey entered the parole board room there were three board members. He remembers them as: an older Latino man who smiled at him, an older white man who "looked like he wanted to be fishing," and a woman with a sour look who waved him to sit down and state his name. Joey claims the men saw his fight at the Sacramento Auditorium. Then the woman went ballistic, "I have read your file and, I too, am from Compton and know all about 18th St. thugs. Just because you are an athlete, do not think you will get treated any different on your incorrigible butt."

Joey says he laughed nervously, realizing he was not likely to be paroled, and was asked if he thought she was funny. "No, but there is no need to talk to me with such vile." He claims the white man wrote down "Dolphins -3, Rams +7, Bears -10."

The female paroler continued, "The new law that has taken affect this year is applicable to you, and under 1170.D and C, an inmate who is found to be incorrigible will be found unsuitable for the Youth Authority and returned to court for sentencing. You, Mr. T-O-R-R-EEEE are incorrigible!"

The Latino man informed Joey that he could appeal the decision and asked if he had anything to say. Joey responded that he understood he had a plea bargain and was told that the longest he would be in prison was when he turned 25. They asked for his Youth Authority ID card as a parting gift, as Joey was being transported back to LA County Jail for re-sentencing.

Joey woke up on the morning of his court date for his modification of sentence. He thought the worst that could happen was 3 more years in prison. Ten people arrived at the Norwalk Superior Court House early on Nov 6, 1982. Joey was appointed another public attorney named James Boedecker, who came to visit him in the holding tank. Boedecker informed Joey that he was in front of a different judge this time. Judge Stevens was not a fan of Joey Torrey and was not going to allow him to withdraw his plea or re-sentence him to three years. The judge was going to allow a plea of second degree murder for 7-10 years with credit for time served.

Joey told Boedecker, "Hell no, buddy. I have a plea agreement and now they want to re-sentence me and I will not plea again!" Joey says Mr. Boedecker assured him he would fight for time served in the appeals court until the end and that was the last time they saw each other before the sentencing.

Joey sat in the holding cell for hours until he was summoned into Judge Steven's court, where the following was recorded by the court:

"Mr. Torrey, I am not going to allow you to withdraw your plea agreement and burden the tax payers of this state with a long drawn out trial. You plead guilty to 187, murder, and in about five minutes, that's what you will be sentenced to. Numerous fights in YA and trying to purchase a gun while in custody. Bad places are for bad people, Mr Torrey, and you're, without a doubt, bad people. Incorrigible is right. Your sentence is just the beginning as the Brigg's initiative just passed on November of 1982, which protects minors, not adults or gangsters like you. You should not have been sentenced to the YA, and I am going to correct that wrong. You could not handle a 3-5 year deal and now you are back."

The judge banged the gavel and asked Joey to stand back as he continued, "I hereby sentence you to 25 years to life in the California Department of Corrections. I will give you credit for 822 days that you served in the Youth Authority."

Court Transcript:

Judge: Do you have further arraignment for judgment?

Boedecker: Yes

Judge: All right. Is there any legal cause why sentence should not be pronounced?

Boedecker: The legal cause has already been stated, as much as the court will allow him to state it.

Judge: All right. Stand up, Mr Torrey. (Defendant complies) For the offense of murder in the first degree, to which the defendant entered a plea of guilty as of January 9, 1980 the defendant is sentenced to the state prison for the term of 25 years to life, with the provision that the defendant is entitled to credit as follows: For a total of 822 days time served in state institutions, including the California Youth Authority, plus 224 days under the provisions of Section 2900.5 of the Penal Code, and an additional 112 days, under the provisions of Section 4019 of the Penal Code. He is remanded to the

Sheriff of Los Angeles County for delivery to the Department of Corrections.

Do you understand that punishment—that penalty?

Torrey: Yes, sir.

Joey says he had to immediately sit down. His knees were buckling. He was escorted out of the court room and met with Mr. Boedecker, who assured him that Judge Stevens sentencing him a second time for the same crime was "double jeopardy." Joey was escorted out, put in shackles, and driven to the Southern Reception Center for the California Department of Corrections in Chino, CA.

That evening, in his cell, Joey heard the paper sliding into his cell that read, "Modification of Sentence: 25 Years to Life." At the bottom it noted his parole eligibility, "June 13, 2002." He says his soul began to rain and thunder as the radio blasted and the screams began. Joey says he did not eat breakfast the following morning. The boxing and cocaine has taken their toll on Joey's brain on top of the fog of events from the day before. An old timer sweeping the floor in front of Joey's cell asked if Joey remembered him from the Main St. gym. Joey did not. That night, the green light was put on the 18th St. gang.

Joey was told to request protective custody from the guards before people returned from lunch, or they were going to be ordered to move on him. Joey had no intention of requesting anything when "this fool from Clanton" stopped at his cell and said, "Lock up! Or when the bars rack, you're dead!" Instead, the lock-up bell rang because someone got stabbed, and they were locked down for the night. Joey loosened up.

Joey skipped breakfast again in the morning, and found himself staring at a long haired biker named Gypsy in front of his cell. Gypsy claimed he was from the Hell's Angels and a friend of Luigi. Joey questioned him until he mentioned 1978, Lancaster, and him beating the ass of one of his bros. Gypsy smiled and extended his hand, explaining that the club is doing business with Luigi and the family, and that he would have Joey's back in the day room. Gypsy told Joey the light was called off as a parting gesture, as someone sent him a message saying "Danny has a knife." Joey felt he had to go to the day room or lose face.

As Joey walked into the day room, he says someone informed him the light was off but that he wasn't going to do anything if it was on. "Bullshit, you fools would have killed me!" Joey says he yelled. He turned on the TV to watch Arguello fight Ganigan as an older man changed the channel. Joey attacked him and a knife clunked to the floor. A biker announced "Let them be." Joey beat him until his hands hurt and kicked the body until his white tennis shoes were covered in blood. Gypsy whispered, "enough," as Joey began pissing on him. An hour later Joey was back in his cell when the guards arrived to put him in solitary confiment.

• • •

Even inside prison, Joey was able to continue using cocaine and was transferred to the mental health unit at Vacaville in 1982. After all of the damage to his brain from cocaine and boxing, he was flagged as mentally unstable.

It was a particularly low point, even for Joey. He worked as a clerk in the Captain's office with receiving and release. Joey settled in—looking forward to his appeal. Technology in medicine was improving and his knee would not need to be replaced.

Charlie Manson was living in the cell block next to Joey's. Charlie would go visiting on the weekend with different women and bring back "screaming weed." Joey says Charlie would play guitar as they sat around and smoked, while Joey drew sports scenes and athletes. Joey figured that Charlie pretended to be crazy. When someone wanted to interview him, he'd look at the guards and declare "showtime!" and make different faces, asking which was the craziest. He would occasionally go from cell to cell, purchasing a TV for anyone who didn't have one.

On October 15 Joey was leaving work at the Captain's office when old time sergeant Richard Barajas pulled him aside and asked him to watch Adela Maria Esparza, a rookie guard being trained, who was assigned to Joey's cell block. He instructed that if she needs help, Joey should look out for her. After a fight in the gym, Joey was headed to take a shower when he heard her screaming. Joey returned to the office to find a crowd of 15-20 inmates yelling, laughing, punching her in the face, and tearing her clothes.

Joey pushed his way through and began beating on one ringleader who had been punching her in the face. Then he picked up a phone and later an old cast iron mop ringer to "baptize" the man beating her. After the man was passed out, Joey scared away the crowd, locked the room, and hit the emergency button. When security arrived, Joey claims that they began beating him after seeing the passed out Esparza. When Officer Esparza finally woke up she told them what had actually happened.

Joey had violated an unwritten rule of the prison. You don't ever side with your captors. Joey was marked—Boxer from 18th with mob ties who never helps his captors, had done exactly that.

Corrections typically keep a list of inmates and their enemies, in order to separate them, but Joey ran into Morgan, who had led the assault on Officer Esparza, the following evening. A shadowy figure attacked Joey from behind. He woke up days later in the Hospital with a plate in his head.

Joey was sent to Vacaville Medical Center and a report was filed by the officer who sent him to protect Ms. Esparza. Joey, wanting to prevent future attacks and to spite the guards, filed a lawsuit over negligence and the scars on his face. The prison system arranged his transfer to California Men's Colony.

He now lived across the hall from Larry Singleton—who had kidnapped a little girl in Riverside, raped and cut off her arms, and left her by a ditch, but was somehow currently being paroled. Joey had read that the girl's family was awarded a million dollars, and when Joey informed Singleton of this, he supposedly replied, "Yeah, but she can't count it."

On Fridays, in his new environment, the Army boxing team would visit the prison gym to box with him. At 23, Joey felt he should have been peaking as a fighter, but his career was shot.

Affidavit of Adela Maria Esparza

I began working at California Medical Facility in Vacaville, CA as a correctional officer on October 8, 1982. My duties included the supervision of inmates classified as psychotics in remission. Before working at CMF, I worked at the California Institute for Men, in Chino, for eighteen months, also as a correctional officer.

I make this statement on behalf of Joey Torres, who saved my life at CMF.

On October 15, 1982, after one week of orientation, I began my first day of supervising Wing P-3 on the psych unit. Shortly after my shift began, an inmate named Thomas Morgan started following me and making comments. Throughout the evening, Morgan became increasingly menacing and bizarre in his behavior toward me. I called his behavior to the attention of my direct supervisor, Sgt. Parker. After a brief meeting, Sgt. Parker determined that Mr. Morgan posed no threat and refused to take any action.

Because Morgan continued in his bizarre behavior, I also advised Officer Barajas (a supervisor of another wing on the same shift) of Morgan's disruptive behavior. Officer Barajas indicated that he would occasionally check to see how I was doing. Officer Barajas said that if I got into trouble, I could count on inmate Torres because, "He is a good inmate." Joey Torres also reassured me that if I got into trouble, he would back me up.

Again, I complained to my supervisor of Morgan's continued and increasingly menacing behavior. I requested Morgan either be moved or locked up in his cell. He denied this request.

At one point, I heard Morgan say under his breath that he was "going to kill" me.

As I began to direct all inmates back into their cells at lock up time, through a pass window, I looked up and the next thing I knew, Morgan punched me in the face with such force that my teeth were loosened, my mouth lacerated and my face bloodied. Morgan came into the room, stood over me, and attempted to hit me again. I was only semi-conscious but managed to kick his groin area and began screaming. He proceeded to attack me again. Although there were a number of inmates surrounding us by that time, only Torres intervened to stop Morgan's attack.

At Chino, the alarm button is located on the hip area. Because I was unfamiliar with the placement of the newer alarm button, I reached for my hip area. Torres yelled out to remind me that the button was located in my chest pocket. I was then able to alert other officers of my need for assistance.

It is my belief that inmate Morgan had every intention of killing me. Had it not been for Torres' intervention. I believe that Morgan would have killed me or caused serious bodily harm. Torres saved my life and averted a potentially volatile situation in which other inmates could have become disruptive.

That evening, I reported the events to Officer Evelyn Mason. She assured me that Torres would get recognition in his file for saving an officer's life. It was not until earlier this year that I become aware that a report of this incident was not placed in his file. I did nothing to identify him or highlight his actions, as I did not want to endanger his safety within the inmate population.

Recently I learned that Torres was severely beaten by inmate Morgan and—as a result of this beating—now wears a steel plate in his head. His attempt at saving my life put his own life in jeopardy and he had to be transferred out of his prison in California to a Nevada facility.

If called as a witness, I can completely testify as to the truth of the foregoing statements.

-Executed this 28th day of November, 1989 at San Francisco, CA. Notarized by the Notary Public.

Ken Hurdle—Statement of Character

August 21, 2002

Correctional Lieutenant Evelyn Mazon wrote, rather than coming to the aid of an injured officer, inmates will usually say they saw nothing. However:

"Inmate Torres came to the aid of another human being, regardless of the consequences. Torres knew that night what would happen to him. He tried to tell me, but I did not understand. Joey said something that night, and years later I understood the full meaning. 'What's going to happen to me, Mazon? I couldn't leave her alone. He is so big and could kill her. I had to do it. What's going to happen to me, Mazon?' As the years have passed, I can now fully appreciate and understand what Torres really did. I have also come to realize that Joey is a very special person. I have never said that about any inmate."

"Being in corrections, I do not get involved with inmates' personal lives and have no feelings, one way or another, about them being in prison. With Joey, I would like to see him get out. Joey did a very good thing and was chastised for his actions. It's time they recognize that Joey will make a good U.S. citizen."

In my opinion, it is the many laudatory comments from corrections officials that are particularly noteworthy.

In July 1993, New Mexico Corrections officials wrote that Mr. Torrey, "spends a considerable amount of time on the phone, either direct or through three way calls, promoting his Boxers Against Drugs program."

Joey contacts numerous sports figures to do personal appearances, card shows, prison visits, autograph signings, and various other things to fight drug abuse. He states he spends up to 10 hours per day on the phone. The expenses *for all the phone work is done through donated monies from athletes and donated signed sports items that can be auctioned off.*

"Joey appears to have a sincere and dedicated attitude towards helping others not make the same mistakes he did."

Clearly these people were moved and impressed by Joey's character but looking at this and the bigger picture of his actions over time, it made me wonder. Morality is the sense that you would save a woman being attacked by a mentally unstable man because it's the "correct" thing to do, but what if your brain worked in ways to identify saving a life as the action that was the "correct" way to get out of prison?

Joey sat in Vacaville segregation with numerous administrators who were facing the federal lawsuit that he had written while sitting in the hole. Joey found it entertaining and easy to litigate the system he was coming to understand. He claims that one night, after numerous beat downs by the guards for his lawsuit, an associate warden came to visit him and finally said, "If you drop the suit they will send you to any other prison in the U.S. that the department has an agreement with."

Joey started writing to Ana Luisa, another old "friend" who was close to Las Vegas and could visit him. Joey sent word to the yard about his return and was sent a message indicating a setup; "Come out to the yard Joey. All is OK." Joey packed his bags for Nevada.

When Joey agreed to be sent out of state, he transferred to Soledad State Prison, in the Protective Housing Unit. It was a special cell block with three front doors in which everyone needed buzzed through. Joey remained there for months—awaiting his ride to Nevada. He was housed with some of the nation's most violent, high profile child molesters and murderers. There was Dan White (who murdered Harvey Milk and San Francisco Mayor Masconi), Juan Corona (who buried a bus full of farm workers), Sirhan Sirhan (who was charged with shooting Robert Kennedy), and numerous gang shot callers who now were informing for their "security."

Joey remembers watching Oliver North testify on TV about Iran/Contra from this cell block. The New York Giants were in the Super Bowl, and Joey was receiving mail and visits from Terry, another old "friend" who he says he decided to marry for the conjugal visits.

Joey was finally transferred in 1986 to maximum security Nevada state prison, located in Carson City. Snow-covered mountains lie beyond this old penitentiary. Joey says he left Terry because "her family lived the gang life," and the association with him put them in danger. So he picked Nevada to be closer to Ana Luisa, a wholesome woman who still lived with her parents.

Joey did not know anyone in Carson City and began a new anonymous life. He watched the playoff baseball game where Billy Buckner, of the Red Sox, allowed a ball to travel between his legs off the bat of Mookie Wilson. Joey smiled when he saw Darryl Strawberry, who he knew as a kid in his old neighborhood. Nevada had a boxing program and Joey would watch the kids bang the bag and spar for hours, but he was afraid to engage them for fear of someone recognizing him as a "cop lover."

•　　　•　　　•

One day, Joey was escorted to see his counselor, who he felt was a nice lady who appreciated him saving the guard. She informed him that she pulled some strings to have him sent to their state's kick back prison. Joey didn't understand, but on January 6, 1987, he was driven towards the California/Nevada border, eventually reaching Jean, NV.

Nestled against a mountain near I-15, it was located behind Pistol Pete's casino—where the Bonnie & Clyde car was housed. Joey saw inmates walking around in personal clothes, wearing baseball jerseys, looking relaxed, and playing golf. Then on the other side of the yard, Joey saw a tennis court, and there in the middle of the yard was a boxing ring!

Inmates walked out. They were virtually all old and white. Joey says he was waiting for food as he watched each inmate make a different special request. Jimmy Sacco appeared with a cigar as big as Luigi's and introduced himself. He went on to say that he was a friend of Luigi's and the family, and that he pulled some strings to get Joey relocated to "Camp Snoopy."

Joey claims that Sacco ran the biggest sports book in the nation. According to Joey, he recently began heading the biggest offshore gambling establishment in Costa Rica.

They ate, and Sacco told Joey who's dead and who's telling. Joey says Jimmy informed him that the Steve's Muffler "issue" was based on money owed to him. Joey claims that the guards came by to slip Jimmy his daily bottle of vodka. Jimmy explained that of the 500 inmates on the yard, half were perverts or molesters, and the other half were slot cheats and white collar criminals like himself. Jimmy was making big money from prison and running his operation in Santo Domingo and Costa Rica from his cell. He supposedly handed Joey a shoe box with a few Cuban cigars, a roll of bills, toothpaste, and odds and ends.

Joey found his cell had wall-to-wall carpeting, a recliner, a giant stereo, TV with cable, and a telephone! In exchange for handing over your ID card, the guards would hand you a phone.

Joey received a knock one morning from Ernie, a guy Joey knew from the Spilotro family. His boss had recently been found buried in a hole in the desert. His crew was known as the "hole in the wall" gang because they entered through one building to rob the adjacent one. He was also a barber who gave a nice cut. They'd smoke cigars and go down memory lane. Joey spent the next day working out, ordering a large cheese pizza and nachos, and watching cable TV in his cell.

Ana Luisa Hernandez visited Joey on Saturdays. He says, "She looked like Dolly's twin—down to her class and old school love and respect for her family." Joey could receive groceries from visitors: avacados, plantains, and quarts of Pepsi half full of Bacardi!

Joey told Jimmy Sacco that he wanted to fight again and get a professional fight under his belt. Sacco told Joey that he was too smart and that they should instead promote other fights. Jimmy floated him a few thousand dollar loan, and Joey went on a phone campaign, learning that the phone can be a powerful tool. Joey called Top Rank's office in Vegas and spoke to Miguel Diaz, an old time trainer who, according to Joey, "betrayed Jimmy Montoya and everyone in his path to become the number one self-proclaimed cut man in boxing."

Joey told Diaz that he needed boxers out at the prison for an exhibition. Top Rank was the same agency who had asked Joey to fight when he was 17.

Next, Joey made an appointment with the warden, Walter Luster, who happened to be a boxing fan himself. Luster was in his 60s, and a part-time boxing coach. Joey asked about his idea of promoting fights from the prison. Luster smiled and said he loved it. Joey called every television station—local and abroad. They were only 35 miles from the Vegas strip.

Joey made a call to John Nadel, of the *Associated Press* in LA He told Nadel about his crime and they struck up a friendship. Joey asked Nadel to get him in touch with Eric David and Darryl Strawberry.

11

Joey says he came to consider Nadel and his daughter like family, and what an opportune family to have. John helped him get ahold of Davis and Strawberry, and Joey invited them to his event. Joey says John would slip him numbers for athletes, and Joey would interview them. He'd ask them to speak to Nadel, and would get a scoop.

One day Joey said he was able to hear sadness in Nadel's voice. Joey asked him what the problem was and learned that his daughter was using methamphetamines or "ice." Over the next few years, Joey would call John's daughter and talk about how drugs had ruined his life and John's daughter Stacy eventually turned her life around and graduated college. Joey was contacted by Fox Television—who wanted to do a special on him.

After being in some of this country's most violent prisons, it was confusing for Joey when the guards and inmates would greet him with "good morning." Joey says he pondered what they wanted from him. Perhaps the way that he looked at the world was tempering his expectations of others and not everyone was working an angle. It's a telling story when you can't even trust those around you to be pleasant for genuine reasons.

Joey saw on ESPN that Len Bias and Don Rogers had died of cocaine overdoes—two young athletes whose lives hadn't really yet begun. Joey had an idea to help young athletes from the inner city to deal with the drug epidemic. He says he loved working with Stacy Nadel and talking to kids in trouble.

Boxers Against Drugs (BAD) was officially created that evening. Joey called his attorney for advice and direction. Joey met with Warden Luster, and within three weeks, they presented a list of visitors for this boxing exhibition. It began with Boom Boom Mancini and went on to include three pages of important figures in the sports and entertainment world. Eric Davis and Darryl Strawberry would drop in on fight night. Joey hired a secretary to keep up with requests from parents and celebrities who sought his help. He remembered Carlos Palomino and called Mr. Nadel, who ran a story about Carlos and Joey. The story went on the news wire, and Joey blew up. The phone kept ringing and ringing.

Joey called Mr. Palomino and asked if he remembered him asking for a shot at his title. Carlos laughed, and Joey told him about his situation. Joey asked Carlos to come to the promotion at the prison and help with the B.A.D. program. Carlos showed up on the first day of his first promotion, explaining, "I wanted to look in his eyes and see if I was hearing the truth or getting conned. We talked for a couple of hours and I felt like he was real." Miguel Diaz brought in five boxers—one Joey was following was Antifoshi, from Nigeria, who was on his way to a title shot.

From Joey's prison cell, B.A.D. reached many children over the next decade with their sports heroes reinforcing the power of family and staying in school. This message was seen worldwide on television, cleverly blending the B.A.D. pitch with that of Joey's innocence. In order to fund the operation, Joey began selling portraits, including one of Darryl Strawberry. With Strawberry's mother, Joey created a t-shirt that her church would sell. Joey claims that he made six figures from selling artwork and reproduction rights from prison that year.

Joey began calling Strawberry and Davis at their homes or hotels on the road. Daryll's brother Ronnie was having drug problems so Joey reached out to him. Darryl himself was partying pretty hard and about to head down a dark road too.

•   •   •

Over the next three years Joey created a network through his relationships with Davis and Strawberry. One of them would either know the player he was trying to get in touch with or Joey could sweet talk them into working with him on the basis of his existing relationships with "Straw" and "E." Joey successfully convinced player after player to sign ten dozen baseballs for him to sell. Joey would have Ana Luisa buy a dozen baseballs for $60, which he had already pre-sold to collectors for $2,000 per dozen.

Joey says he did this everyday—with five to ten players per week. It was 1986, now known as the hottest time in history for sports memoribilia. Joey would coordinate moving cars for players down to Florida for them to use during spring training. Eventually Davis would be calling Joey from Atlanta to ask for help getting a breakaway back board installed in his backyard. Joey claims he would call Reebok, convince them to pay for it, and pocket all of the cash. If he has no qualms admitting that he was performing these relatively sketchy moves on his rich "friends," one might wonder what kind of books were cooking in the B.A.D. accounting.

When Carlos Palomino visited Joey during this period he described that it felt like the guards were working for Joey, coming by to check in on them periodically, asking if either of them needed anything else. He says it didn't feel like prison.

•　　　•　　　•

In 1998 Joey was again summoned to the warden's office. There, he found his father looking old and forlorn. His clothes hung loosely, like they belonged to someone else. The warden walked out and Joey's father informed him that both he and Joey's mother had cancer. His father had lung cancer and his mother had cancer of the blood.

Supposedly, his father told him about watching his fights and wanting Joey to lose, "You were the fighter that I could never be and a father should not be jealous of his own son, but I was."

Joey's father moved to Vegas and Joey tried to be closer to both parents. He had baseball players call his dad, mail him signed bats and balls, and had Darryl and Eric invite him to a Dodgers' game.

Joey's mother remained in the hospital with a rare blood disorder. The doctor did not expect her to live more than three or four days. Joey called Carlos Palomino who contacted the California Department of Corrections. Joey explained to director Jim Gomez's secretary, "I am in another state for saving the life of a correctional officer and I want a chance to kiss my mother before she passes." Finally, hours later, Joey claims Gomez allowed him to visit his mother with the warning,

"I am letting you go free for the day but if you run I will hunt you down!" And to his credit, it was one of the only opportunities to flee the authorities that Joey did not take.

This is quite an exception as the law stated, "no convicted murderer will be released into society for any reason." Joey headed to LA with Palomino where he found his mother in a coma distressingly hooked into numerous machines. She passed away the next day after Joey had returned to prison.

•   •   •

Joey claims he began producing the TV show *Rapamania* as a coping mechanism for his mother's death. He claims an attorney named Steve Shiffman, Carlos, and Harold Lipton asked him to promote the pay per view show where the country's top hip hop artists performed. Joey claims he made a million dollars in 1988 and spent it all on clothes for other people's kids.

If the Reds were in New York Joey would call the Mets public relations department and claim to represent Eric Davis, requesting his hotel number. He'd ask Eric to tell Bobby Bonilla to expect his call. He convinced Eric to collect all the broken bats and equipment he could gather and leave it at the front desk where Joey would have FedEx pick it up the next day to send to a baseball shop that Joey had already sold it to that morning. If someone needed cars moved, tickets obtained, or jewelry bought, Davis would send them to Joey.

Joey claims he was taking bets from Pete Rose, who would bet with the bookie, sending the money back to Jimmy Sacco. Joey claims Pete, as the Reds' coach, would also connect him with players who needed tasks performed.

A week after the holidays of 1988 when Carlos Palomino was asked about Joey's prison cell management operation, Joey was featured on the *George Michael Sports Machine*, *Fox Television*, *The Reporters*, and *A Current Affair*. Joey started receiving bags of mail and was introduced to Youth Development, Inc. (YDI) in Albuquerque—a model of what a national program could be. They worked with gang kids, found jobs, did education, and housed single mothers. Joey spent the next few years working under director Chris Baca, who became something of a mentor.

Joey claims he was paying $3,000 per month in phone bills, callling Japan to get card show appearances for players he represented, calling players daily for bats and balls, and calling his dad to cheer him up.

Joey managed to "befriend" Edward James Olmos shortly after his Oscar-winning performance in *Stand and Deliver,* who also came to vocally defend Joey's "right" to be released.

Joey was making "so much money" that he sent 200 kids to Magic Mountain, sent bikes to a Christmas program, and hired a new appeals attorney, Cheryl Lutz. Melvin Belli was pursuing a governor's pardon from governor Pete Wilson, which went downhill after Belli began telling the media that the governor should be put into the bay on a boat without paddles. So Joey began reading law books at the end of his work day.

Joey's dad mentioned that Paul Molitor of the Baseball Hall of Fame was Puerto Rican. Joey tracked him down and he happened to see the *Sports Machine* episode about Joey but explained that he was actually French Canadian.

Joey found that the players who grew up in poverty surrounded by a gang climate tended to cling to him better than those who were born better off. Eric Davis, interviewed during Joey's roughest period, said simply "Joey is my friend."

Joey became so close with Paul Molitor that he was credited with help talking Paul through a hitting slump.

But in another seemingly fickle spate of leaving his girlfriend and life behind, Joey decided to request a transfer to New Mexico to be closer to YDI. It was 1990 by the time Carlos let him know his transfer was approved. Joey owed Sacco $50,000, who reportedly laughed it off and let it go, so Joey says he sent Sacco a "donation" every week thereafter.

And so when Mr. Lipton attempted not to pay Joey for *Rapamania*, he and Quimby Jones were supposedly visited by Mr. Gambino, who "made them see Jesus," whatever that might mean, since they were still alive.

Joey found the state pen in Santa Fe to be like a John Wayne movie. The former gas chamber room was intact and there remained burn marks from efforts to burn out the last inmate during a riot. It is also where *Dig's Town* and *The Longest Yard* were filmed.

Athletes remained willing to travel to Albuquerque in support of Joey's message of hope for kids. Joey says he convinced Emmitt Smith to make a personal appearance for YDI after obtaining some $2,000/case of rare Upper Deck cards for Emmitt's father. Emmitt flew out, did a fundraiser for YDI, and signed hundreds of iron-on number "2"s and 8x10"s, which Joey sold for $400 each as his own fundraiser. Since Albuquerque had no sports teams, the Dallas Cowboys were treated like a local.

Joey created a radio show from the prison station called *Sports Talk with Joey T*. His first interview was with Eric Davis and Daryl in rehab.

Joey says he worked producing the rap group Lynch Mob, who supposedly asked him to sell cases of glock 9mm handguns and hand grenades that they had stolen during the LA riots to pay for their recording time. Apparently, in Joey's identity, that didn't contradict the image he had built up with B.A.D., but he does claim there was some matter of conscience. When the California Department of Corrections refused to pay him for the weapons, he handed them over to the ATF. Again, he says he expected this would put a gold star on his record and help him get out of prison, which it did not. Joey's self-image remained complicated and seemingly incongrous. Even when he re-tells the stories now, he seems to be creating contradictory and revisionist history as he goes.

•   •   •

One day he was called to the warden's office while he was in the middle of making a deal. While it may not have felt like prison to visitors, there remained occasional reminders.

As Joey sat down he says the secretaries asked him for Emmitt stuff, which Joey tended to refuse giving to cops and guards. The new warden supposedly informed Joey, "If you want to keep running your operation, you are going to need to make a donation to my son's baseball team." All calls to and from the prison were recorded so the warden knew exactly how much money Joey was earning behind bars so lying wasn't an option, for once.

Joey says he responded, "Since you broke the ice, I need to be on that same level" leaning forward over the desk. "I will not be sending your son a dime and if anything happens to me, you'll be guaranteed to be cut up into little pieces and put out in the desert." And with that, Joey walked out, smiling. He had been "reformed" to look after his own interests.

After that, Joey was promoting the event of his life—a *Night of the Champions* signing that included Cecil Fielder, Jeff Bagwell, Carlos Palomino, Bip Roberts, Boom Boom Mancini, Scott Cooper, and many more. Lou Gagliano, an associate of "the family," would hand Joey's phone call around from player to player as they signed and then to check the money count. Joey says he chargd $45 for signing flat items and $75 for round items.

He put Ana Luisa in charge of his new company OG Collectibles, which he claims meant "originally guaranteed," because he had letters of authenticity for even the signings he admitted were bogus.

Joey married Ana Luisa that April, and she started to ask about Joey's appeal. Joey thought about it for days. He had created a comfortable life in prison with some fame and a healthy pile of cash. At the same time, he says he felt stupid for sitting in an empty cell while his wife was on the outside.

The same week he'd demanded money from Joey, the prison warden was arrested for soliciting an underage prostitute. Joey's cell door came to be open 24 hours/day on the honor system. He could spend up to 10 hours/day on the phone and Joey used every second. Joey claimed that he paid the guards for a weekly pizza, gold chain, a Rolex, and a bottle of Hennessy. Nonetheless, Joey told Ana Luisa that he would shift focus to his appeal in the prison law library.

After eighteen years of incarceration, Joey came to believe that attorneys represent you as long and as well as you can afford, and their opinions aren't of much importance. Joey had also learned in business that anything is possible, even when he's told that everything is in the hands of the parole board.

Joey met with Chris Baca and informed him of his plans to return to California for access to California law books. Baca understood and wrote letters of support.

Joey contacted Curt Rost from the DOC, explaining his interest in returning to California to appeal his case. Rost understood the dilemma: Joey didn't want to be killed by California inmates but he wanted access to California legal documents to secure his released. Joey was transferred to Folsom Prison while OJ Simpson was all over the television after his wife had been murdered. Being escorted over to the attorney area, Joey claims he ran into two suits he thought looked like Feds.

He took a seat as the suits requested the relationship between Michael Irvin of the Cowboys and Daryl Strawberry's drug connection. The men suggested that they could make it rough for Joey but he claims he said that if he gave them anything on Luigi and Mr. Gambino, it would be worse. Jimmy "the Weasel" Fratianno had turned into a federal informant, sending numerous leads down the chain. Joey claims he said, "There's nothing you could do to me that has not already been done. Fuck you in your Mormon neck."

Joey was informed at his classification hearing that based on his notoriety for saving the female correctional officer he would not be housed at Folsom. He was instead transported to the Maximum Security Housing Protective Unit in Corcoran, a unit full of complaints of sexual abuse, beatings issued by guards and inmates, and staged fights setup by guards, eventually becoming the subject of an episode of *60 Minuites*.

After years in Nevada and New Mexico, Joey was not prepared for this kind of treatment. Joey claims he had two friends in there; Charles Manson and Big C. Big C had been first round football draft pick who kidnapped a college professor for giving him a bad grade. He was serving the 35th year of his sentence of 7-life.

In May of 1996, after 17 years of incarceration, Joey came to devour case law books at all hours of the day and he found out that his father was about to pass away. This time the DOC would not release him to see his father. Joey called Ana Luisa, who put him through to Carlos, who instructed Joey to call in a favor from Gomez. Joey claims that Gomez sent one of his men to pretend to be the warden while special agents escorted Joey in a car to kiss his dad goodbye.

•   •   •

Joey spent the next three years studying law to find an angle to work in his case. Joey began taking work researching cases for other inmates. Out of money after a card show Joey promoted that turned into a bust, Mike Sadek from the Giants was convinced to send Joey signed Willie Mays balls that he would exchange for law books. Paul Moitor would send money from time to time. Joey admits he even traded pornographic pictures of prisoner's wives and sisters to afford his legal forms. Ana Luisa's supported him by scouring the fledgling internet for case history.

The real warden took some inmates off the prison bus from Lancaster one day and beat them to the ground while cutting off their hair and braids. Two guards tossed Joey's cell one day supposedly pocketing a Roberto Clemente card. They were angry that Joey refused to participate in their staged fights. Now 37 and 230 pounds, Joey was physically shot. The guards began telling Ana Luisa that Joey had been transferred when she tried to visit.

Shortly after an ambulance was brought on site by a captain before a staged fight that ended with the guards shooting a prisoner, the *60 Minutes* expose broke and the California DOC was in the national spotlight for its staged fights, beatings, and worse. The department responded by passing a new law that forbid California inmates from talking to the media. Joey was transferred to Soledad.

Joey ran into his childhood friend Lil' Boxer, who was working at the law library there. Lil' Boxer got Joey a job as a library clerk. He was now a shot caller with keys.

Joey saw the doctor and learned he had far-advanced Hepatitis C. He started chemo, which made walking up the stairs a struggle. Getting sick and losing weight, Joey asked Lil' Boxer to watch his back.

One day Joey was called out to the yard by some bikers. He brought Lil' Boxer and some 18th boys out with him. Gypsy walked up to Joey and asked a question as he rolled his head to the right. It was a setup and Joey felt a hot pain in his side. Another fist came and as Joey tried to fight back, his medication knocked him out. Two years later Gypsy was found murdered in his cell. No one came forward to take credit for that one.

The day after getting knifed in his side, Joey went back to work on studying his case. The cops locked down the yard when they found the bloody knife and went cell to cell, looking for wounds. Joey says he buried himself in his books, asked them to leave, and they slammed the door without checking him. Joe returned to the back of the law library and found new laws President Clinton had signed pertaining to appeals and time limitations. Lil' Boxer shook his head in disbelief, looked at the knife wound, which looked like a "blue, black, and red dart board with a pencil-sized hole." Joey hoped there wasn't internal bleeding.

A month later Joey found an old law book and learned about *a writ of error coram nobis* which allows for a review and re-trial if a defendant can prove he wasn't made aware of all possible outcomes before he pleaded guilty. Joey felt this challenged Clinton's bill, which stated an inmate had only a year to appeal a conviction.

Joey told Ana Luisa about his law discoveries and began approaching the press. Joey contacted every attorney in the law directory and was visited by Gary Diamond, an appeals specialist who requested $20,000 to take the case.

Joey also received two letters from James Gallo, a real estate attorney from Pasadena who wanted to help. Next he got a response from Christopher Morales from San Francisco, who graduated UCLA and was a former amateur boxer. The three men would be Joey's team.

Morales investigated the mechanics of *coram nobis* and Gallo would help Joey file motions. Joey says Morales challenged him daily to be his best. Months of prison lockdown from another North/South war gave Joey time to study.

The lawyers gave the thumbs up and Ana Luisa filed Joey's *writ of error coram nobis* on January 8, 2001. She hand delivered it to the clerk in Norwalk. The motion was actually filed seventeen times and each time it came back denied. As each one was denied, Joey put another in the mail. Joey assumed he could challenge the life sentence on account of his plea agreement with the Youth Authority.

He turned on the TV one morning and saw the planes crash into the World Trade Center. The alarm went off, the National Guard took off, and the prison operated on a skeleton crew. Then mail stopped appearing as a result of the anthrax scare. Not even legal mail was delivered for weeks.

Eventaully Mr. Gallo instructed Joey to write an appeal that was less than 100 pages, as that was likely why they were denied. Joey wrote a ten page version.

One day, in his cell, Joey heard chains slamming on the floor and looked up from his bunk to see five transportation guards stopping in front of his cell. As they put the chains around his body Joey suspected someone had mentioned the stabbing or something else he'd done. Little did he know that his appeal had been granted.

13

The medical department began attending to Joey's badly-infected stab wound while he ate a Big Mac. He thought the cars looked like something from the future and marveled at a guard's cell phone.

Ana Luisa was in shock and could not speak. Joey instructed her to buy him some clothes and to rent an apartment for them.

The following morning Joey found himself in the same court room he stood in 20 years earlier. He saw Ana Luisa behind him, looking scared. Joey sat alone, with no attorney next to him, but plenty of bold optimism.

Judge Thomas McKnew, a balding man in his 60s, walked into the court room. He glanced down at Joey's legal briefs. The DA, Pamela Frohreich, began throwing cases, cites, and arguments against Joey. Joey responded, quoting law dating back to King James. After their summations, the Judge returned to his chamber. The bailiff supposedly informed Joey that he had done "a remarkable job." James Gallo showed up to mention Joey's "good behavior" in prison.

An hour later there were keys jingling and butterflys in Joey's stomach like he experienced before a fight. The judge entered and everyone stood.

The stoic judge began reading: "Despite vehement opposition from the District Attorney's Office, Petitioner's petition for writ of *coram nobis* is *granted.*"

Joey had tears in his eyes. Ana Luisa is bug-eyed in shock. Frohreich jumped to her feet in protest.

"The judgment of conviction is hereby vacated, as is petitioner's guilty plea. Petitioner is remanded to custody without bond and shall appear on December 27, 2001."

Joey's sentence was vacated like it had never happened. He was re-arrested for the crime of 1979, like it had never occurred. The penal code stated that applicable bail would be what it was for murder in the first degree in 1979. Joey smiled, appreciating his natural proclivities as a lawyer. Mr. Gallo filed a bail motion to Judge McKnew with a motion for the Department of Corrections to release their hold.

"Mister Torrey, how do you plead to murder in the first degree?"

"Not guilty, your honor."

"I vacate your original sentence but the DA has filed new charges against you because there is no statute of limitations on capital murder. She protested my decision to the court of Appeals, saying I'm not competent to do my job. Now, let's discuss bail."

District Attorney: *"Your Honor, this is a capital murder, in the first degree, as you correctly stated. Therefore, there is no bail, nor has there been since 1980."*

But Joey's crime was in 1979. He is intstructed to debate this action by the DA.

Torrey: *Your honor, I filed a motion on this very subject last night after years of researching. You should have it in front of you. Under the California penal code Sub Sec A6, bail rights are applicable to what they were at the time of the crime, and at no time issuance will be different, based on the fact that the DA was fully correct in stating that as of 1980, no bail on murder one. Ergo, my charged allegations transpired in 1979, one year prior to the law cited.*

Joey says he surprised himself with his grasp of the law and looked triumphantly at the flustered district attorney. The judge looked at his paperwork and raised his eyebrows at the prosecution. The district attorney said, "Your honor, you can't do this. This man was released on a *writ of coram nobis* from a life sentence and now you're going to let him out on bail?"

Judge said, "Yes, I am. What was bail in 1979?"

Joey replied, "One hundred thousand dollars, on a million dollar bond, your Honor."

"Then that's what your bail is today. Good luck, Mr. Torrey." The Judge banged his gavel and left the bench. Pamela Frohreich's face was red with anger.

Joey would receive a new trial and was returned to the holding tank where the bailiff supposedly tipped him off, "The DA is going to request an order to stay your bail. You have 24 hours or you'll remain in custody."

Joey called Ana Luisa, who was still amazed and very quiet. She didn't have a hundred thousand dollars. Joey called Eric Davis, but he was in the Bahamas. Then Paul Molitor. It was midnight in Minnesota where he lived. Joey already owed him $10,000 but says that before he finished his sentence, Molitor said he just needed to figure out how to get the cash.

In an interview at the time, Paul Molitor said, "He was doing good things in prison. It was the right thing to do."

Mr. Gallo had two guys that owned a bond company and secured Joey's release through Molitor's credit card. Joey couldn't sleep that night. In the morning the sergeant asked for his name, number, and if he wanted to go "home." Joey was unsure if it was the latest episode of his 20-year old dream. Mr. Gallo insisted that Joey be released in the evening of January 6, 2002 while the LA County Jail was quiet and everyone was sleeping.

The only clothes available for Joey were Huggy Bear bell bottom pants and a t-shirt. The guards nervously watched the rare instance of an inmate being released after 22 years. Joey gave Mr. Gallo a big bear hug. Walking away from the LA County Jail, Joey said it still felt like a dream.

Mr. Gallo informed Joey, as they climbed into Gall's Benz, that he had called Ana Luisa and she was waiting for them at the old restaurant; The Pantry. Ana Luisa sat alone in a back booth, still looking scared. Mr. Gallo seemed happier than she was that Joey was free.

Joey asked Ana what was wrong and started to get angry. It would seem that Ana Luisa was more secure with Joey in prison. Her life had a comfortable order that way. She advocated Joey's release, but might have been happier if he never got out, regardless of what she had said on the subject.

Gallo left and Ana Luisa was still timid when she asked, "What are we going to do?" Joey felt that she had never quite believed that he would get free. As a result, they spent the rest of the night looking for a hotel room.

The following morning Joey felt like a kid in a candy store. He bought a 40 oz. of De Malt Liquor, a can of Skoal chew and several candy bars at the gas station.

They drove up Highway 101 in silence, holding hands. Living in hotels for the forseeable future, and having trouble finding any that weren't sold out, Joey was getting pissed thinking that if she had listened to him they would have a home to go to.

As they reached the Pacific Coast Highway, the sun was rising—a sight Joey hadn't seen since he was on the beach with JoJo over 20 years previous. Finally they gave up, turned around, and checked into the Holiday Inn on Sunset Blvd. They marvelled at the view from the 20th floor.

The following morning, Joey awoke alone. Ana Luisa had apparently never told her family about him, let alone that she was married to him. So she disappeared in the middle of the night. Even at 29 years old, Ana Luisa was brought up in a culture close-knit to her family.

Lacking a car or even ID, Joey spent his day drinking on the 20th floor. He called Eric Davis who rushed over to drink with him. Eric gave him five grand and a leather coat.

Joey next called Paul Molitor and thanked him.

In the morning, Ana Luisa returned for breakfast and took Joey to obtain his birth certificate, and a driver's license.

Joey spent the next night at his sister's in Santa Clarita. Chris Morales paid for Joey's hotel for a couple weeks and informed him that the DA's office was appealing his release. "Enjoy it while you have it! UCLA has a great law library."

Joey let loose one day on Ana Luisa while they were eating breakfast at the weigh station in Saugus. Ana Luisa had done everything demanded of her for years. She even showed up daily at his hotel room with coffee in hand for him—but this relationship did not resemble a partnership. Joey was mean and lost his temper. Unfortunately, Joey didn't see things this way or understand until she walked out on him for good.

Joey was driven to visit Carlos Palomino, who was working with kids at the boxing gym in Van Nuys. He was greeted by Carlos like a long lost brother. Joey started training and sparring at the Olympic gym and felt the bounce return to his legs. He says it was here that he felt he wanted to commit to having one professional fight.

Not having anyone to pay for his $100/night hotel room anymore, Joey resigned to move into a Holiday Inn in his old neighborhood. Joey was free but alone. He knew how to network but not how to relate with someone as an equal; as a friend. He would run, hit the gym on Olympic, then run back to his hotel room. One day, seeing a 1976 Toyota convertible for sale, he called Paul Molitor and asked him to put that on his credit card as well. Shortly thereafter, in what probably violated the terms of his bail, Joey put the top down and hit the highway.

14

It was a cold day when Joey drove into Las Vegas. He had spent the last two nights in Barstow, holed up in another filthy hotel with a bottle of Hennessy. He would be visiting Miguel Diaz in Vegas, who sounded happy to see him. Miguel sat Joey down in his office and proceeded to go down memory lane.

Joey closed the door and told him, in all seriousness, that he wanted to return to the ring at 42 years old. Diaz smiled and called in Bruce Trampler who told Joey that he was crazy, but asked for a few days to clear it through his boss, boxing legend Bob Arum. Trampler was the primary matchmaker for Top Rank who Joey had already been in touch with from prison. Trampler apparently saw the angle of a chubby ex-con in a Hawaiian shirt as a comeback kid in a hard-luck fairy tale for the everyman.

Miguel hit the intercom for his secretary Angie, who turned out to be the same Angie from the Forum Boxing Club in Inglewood, CA. Angie gave Joey a key and a room to stay in on Flamingo Blvd. Joey's phone rang and it was Sean Gibbons, Trampler's assistant, who came by to pick him up.

Around 10 p.m. Gibbons unlocked the Top Rank office, and sat behind Mr. Arum's desk, supposedly laying out lines of coke, and inviting Joey to join him. He opened a bottle of Captain Morgan and they sat, did lines, and drank. After awhile, they moved the party to Trampler's office.

Sean, known by boxing insiders as "Buddy Holly" (for his resemblance) or "The Oklahoma Meat Packer" (for his boxing management style), supposedly snorted more coke, and promised to take Joey to meet Bob Arum in the morning.

Joey received a call that night from Angie, who instructed him not to trust Sean. Angie, as it turned out, also knew Eric

Davis and his crew. Joey believes she was the only honest person involved with Top Rank.

The next morning, Sean woke Joey up, banging on his door, with a bag full of food, coke, Hennesy, and papers in hand. Alert and seemingly full of coke, Sean walked in, poured a drink, and smiled. Somehow, Sean had a wife and two kids.

As Sean ran down the score, Joey mentioned concern about a four fight deal, thinking he was only good for one. Sean supposedly broke it down, "I'm the fixer—you could walk in the ring blindfolded and still win. Arum will have money invested in you by then and will demand that you win every fight. I'm called in to make sure that happens. Don't worry!" Supposedly Sean told Joey that he had men who'd lie down in a fight for a bottle of Tequilla, with the fights being pre-scripted.

Mr. Arum was not available for their meeting, so Joey sat in an office with Bruce Trampler. He liked Bruce, who seemed more concerned about his welfare than boxing. According to Joey, when push came to shove, Trampler ran Top Rank and was in an ongoing power struggle with Arum's stepson for managerial control of the company.

Joey put Trampler in touch with the state appointed attorney handling his appeal, Verna Wefald. Joey had met with her once before heading to Vegas and felt she was his ticket to staying out of prison.

The following morning, Sean picked Joey up to meet with Bob Arum. The meeting was scheduled for 10 a.m. and Bob waved Joey to sit, and then informed him, *You will be fighting on the 23rd of April, at the Anaheim Pond. Here is $5,000 to buy some clothes.* Arum told Joey that they would talk to the media together, representing Top Rank, and supposedly also, "Do not worry about winning the fight, but lose some weight to resemble a boxer."

Joey says Angie kept him abreast of who was in his corner. Trampler seemed to be the one making things happen for Joey. Joey says he only saw Arum at press conferences or when he pushed around Arum's stepson. With Bruce in Joey's corner, it was in his best interest to push around Bruce's managerial rival.

Sean became Joey's manager and Joey claims he pushed Sean for the next 500 days to go to the gym, lose weight, and train for the fight. Instead, he claims Sean was setting up other fights and finding people to take falls go up against boxers who couldn't be beat. Joey claims there was an elaborate system of people who came to town, partied with the crew, stayed in cheap hotels, were knocked out, and headed home to spend the money buying more drugs.

After the office would close, Joey says he would party with Sean and some "victims" before their losing fights. After they were properly coked up, Joey claims they would walk over to the strip. One night, Luigi told Joey to stay away from The Crazy Horse "Gentleman's Club." But Joey didn't listen and headed over with Sean. At the entrance to The Horse stood Bubbles the bouncer, who recognized Joey. Bubbles had worked for Uncle Frank in 1977 in Lancaster, Californi at the pizzeria.

Inside the strip joint, another bouncer requested $100 for lap dances and drinks as they sat down. Sean pulled out the money but Joey got up to leave and Sean followed him out. Bubbles asked if there was a problem as the other bouncer moved behind Joey. Joey claims the Crazy Horse was the kind of place that if you did not pay your bill or ten times your bill, you'd have an "accident" on the way out.

After Bubbles' interjection, Joey claims the Horse's prices either weren't charged or were very reasonable, but unbeknown to them, in the midst of their debauchery, someone was watching from a Ford Escort across the street. Bubbles, without a second look said "FBI," and Sean was quiet for the first time since Joey had met him. They hid out in VIP, drinking till the early morning, when Bubbles got off work. Before leaving, Bubbles asked Joey, "You okay, Luigi's brother?"

They walked out as the sun was rising over the Tropicana. Joey knew the Feds were watching the place so he stayed away for awhile and went to Spearmint Rhino instead, among the "common folks." Joey met a woman named Octavia who he said made him laugh, saying he "related to her hustle."

Like JoJo, Emma, and Sonya, Octavia was another prostitute, and "one of the most genuine people" he had ever met. A former underwear model, Joey says Octavia claimed to make $2,000-3,000 per job.

Sean seemed to buy into the hype that Joey wrapped around himself and began repeating it around Vegas. The doors that were once closed, were now open and inviting.

New women kept ringing Joey's new cell phone. Joey has a knack for meeting women—especially prostitutes—giving them his phone number and enough incentive to call him, losing interest as they gain it, and then telling the story in a way that the responsibility of the situation falls far from his own shoulders. Perhaps Joey says it best: "[I] did not know how to appreciate a tender loving person. I put moments of pleasure in front of a lifetime of love."

Joey started to do promotions for other Top Rank Boxing matches. He claims Top Rank had Kevin Iole, a reporter for the *Review Journal* on the payroll. Kevin wrote a three page cover story on a Sunday about Joey. It's one of the few pieces of media that paints a positive, albeit, one-sided, picture of Joey.

Top Rank's PR machine was in full force and turned Joey into an overnight celebrity, despite being 42 years old and overweight. They began having Joey appear to glam up Friday night fights. As Gibbons took a liking to Joey, he used Joey as his personal muscle and gofer while Trampler attempted to forge a new screenwriting talent, with visions of turning Joey's life into a movie.

Joey asked Octavia to lease him a CK 55 Benz Convertible, with the AMG package, sitting on spinners, for his birthday. She did. He would park it with the casino valet who would detail it while he gambled. Instead of training, Joey claims he was drinking one gallon rum and cokes, swimming in the pool, making calls, and tanning.

Top Rank hired another new publicist—Lee Samuels— who arranged a photo shoot for Joey before he left for Livermore, California with Top Rank.

Joey had a 1 p.m. meeting with Bob Arum the following day. Having nowhere else to go, Joey arrived at noon and walked into Top Rank with baskets of cookies and candies. He walked up behind Angie, kissed the top of her head while she was on the phone, and put a basket in front of her.

When they finally sat down to their meeting, Joey says Arum declared *Bruce Trampler said we can promote one hell of a show with you, call it "the come back!"* Joey says he smiled and explained, "Sir, I am 42 years old and have not fought in years." Supposedly, Arum smiled, chuckled, looked over at Bruce and stated, "Kid, you just show up and your opponents will fall when told. Don't worry about that."

While most of the boxing business establishment before him consisted of black men like Don King or were associated with established organized crime, Bob Arum is a Jewish man who was born into relative wealth. A former attorney for Senator Kennedy, he has contracts with Telefutura, a Spanish TV network, ESPN, and pay-per-view. He brings new fighters to market by bringing them up in ratings on Spanish television before being brought to pay-per-view in the U.S. It was Sean's job to make sure to "secure the investment."

The fight in Livermore was to take place at an Indian Casino. Joey was handed credentials and asked to walk the fighter into the blue corner. He says the winning Top Rank fighters were always in the red corner and they'd usually keep the same coach in the blue corner all night long.

Joey sat in Trampler's hotel room as they ran down the operation. Joey claims Trampler was connected to the New York mob family, which further increased respect he had for Bruce's professional acumen. They became "close" and that closeness seemed to get Joey all of the favors that Top Rank did for him. As they were chatting after the fight, Sean summoned Joey to room 344.

In room 344 Joey says he found some girls having sex with up-and-coming boxers. Joey claims he saw Top Rank attorney Scott Woodworth cutting fifty or so coke lines. Scott had been an attorney for Don King and had managed Terry Norris to win the WBC Junior Middleweight. Scott introduced Joey to his brother Ryan, whom Joey had already met as a prisoner in Soledad. Scott complained that Todd Debouf was pressuring Mr. Arum to have him fired.

Scott asked Joey to sit down and supposedly said "Fuck Top Rank. I will handle your comeback and will give you half a million to fight Orlin Norris for a bogus title that you will win." Sean shrugged his shoulders. Top Rank was only paying Joey $20,000.

Joey returned to Vegas in the morning with Sean. Scott went back to San Diego. Sean informed Joey that Scott was going to be fired that week for contract mistakes that cost Top Rank around one million dollars. Joey sent Octavia to find him a new residence for the two of them and flew to San Diego to meet with Scott.

At the airport Joey says he ran into Ken Hurdle from the California DOC, who he explained his good fortune to. Scott was out front with a limo for Joey. They hugged and were off to Scott's home where they read the press about Joey's upcoming fight. Scott had been fired that morning and had spent the day making a banner that declared "Training Center for Joey Torrey. Unfinished Business." with matching 8x10" photos. Scott put up Joey in a San Diego hotel with a balcony overlooking the ocean.

Joey says that Scott knocked on the door, slumped in a seat, yelling on the phone to Todd Debouf from Top Rank, "Well fuck you too, punk!," and poured a vial of coke onto the table. The more Joey interacted with Scott, the more he felt that Scott may have been using more cocaine than anyone else at Top Rank.

Joey says that Scott claimed he was connected to the family through David Gambino in San Diego and one of the boss' sons was living in La Jolla, bank-rolling his new promotional firm. Joey's return to the ring would be the company's first promotion for The Entertainment King. Joey felt Scott was increasingly becoming a loose cannon.

Joey called Luigi, asking about The Entertainment King. Luigi started to laugh, saying that he was asked about the same man a few weeks earlier and the kid was not a "made" guy, friend, or associate, but his family had money.

Joey asked Luigi for advice, who told him to get back to Vegas and show some respect to Trampler for what he'd done for Joey. Joey says when Scott called from downstairs with The Entertainment King, Joey cleaned his steak knife and placed it in his waist band.

Joey went downstairs and saw two men in the dark bar plus Scott, and this short, dark kid sitting at a table. The door guys wore pressed suits with gold chains from the disco era. Joey smiled, approached Scott, and looked into the eyes of the 25 year old kid. After ten minutes of Scott talking up the praises of the kid Ralph, Joey said "I need some good faith money in order to turn my back on Top Rank. Fifty grand would be some real good faith."

Ralph said that money is no problem and he owns two strip joints in San Diego and his family was going to make this happen. Joey claims he said, "Entertainment King, What family? You're not even Italian. You're Armenian on a school Visa and your parents are throwing money at you. This guy at the bar and these guys at the door better be packing because I will slide this steak knife in your eye socket, you fraud." As an Armenian, Ralph was not eligible to be part of the "family." Ralph walked out and Joey told Scott he was returning to Vegas in the morning.

•　　•　　•

Joey admits that he finds joy in manipulating the minds of people who pretend to be gangsters. He feels that his street activities and time in prison give him a right to "feel people out" in this way, but it would seem to also indicate a joy of being in control, of calling the shots. As he says "If you're not [gangster], I will fuck with your mind all night till you fight or pull me aside and admit you are a coward that loved watching *Scarface*."

Joey says he felt "funny" about embarrassing Scott for being tricked by this kid, so they went back to Joey's room, did more lines of coke, and ordered room service. It was almost like a moment of empathy.

Before Joey headed back to Vegas he ordered a bottle of rum to the pool. He checked his phone and says he had thirty new messages. As he was listening to them, Sean called, saying Trampler was pissed, Arum wants Joey to call him, and Sean's loyalty is to Top Rank. Joey said, "Relax fool. I'll be back tonight." When Trampler called a minute later, Joey says he interrupted him, "I'll see you at the office in the morning. I needed to get away and take care of some business." Joey headed down to the pool with his $500 bottle of rum.

In Joey's version of events, as the pool gates opened, two men wearing Hawaiian shirts, shorts, and black socks with dress shoes walked in. Joey thought they were Feds based on their hairstyles and keptness. They sat next to Joey and read the paper. As Joey got up, he says one of the men asked if he was Joey Torrey. Joey replied in the affirmative and they identified themselves as FBI, Organized Crime Division.

"We know you're fighting for Top Rank and we know your fight is fixed. We've been bugging their office for years but could never get anyone in close. We also know that you are out of prison on appeal bond and have a pretty wife. Where's that pretty wife of yours?" The other Fed chimed in, "I have been working in Oklahoma, trying to get Sean since he had the Knucklehead Boxing Club with Pete Sousa." Joey says he was all ears, "tripping big time" as they went on.

Joey ordered another whiskey and claims they said, "Prove your fight is fixed and you will get what you want. The appeal will never happen. We spoke to the D.A. and she is going to appear to fight it, but let you plead to time served. Otherwise, you're going back to prison for life. The U.S. government is willing to protect you, whether you testify or not."

Joey says he was speechless as they handed him a business card, saying, "I'm sure glad you didn't put that knife in that kid's eye. You have 24 hours and Washington needs to know."

Joey kept the FBI's card in his shoe, where he wouldn't need to explain it to anyone. He went back to his room looking through his clothes for bugs. Then he wondered what the hell to do. Joey felt that he had no one he could talk to about this offer—not his brother, not Trampler, not even his attorney, who was a specialist at going after the FBI. The hotel phone rang. It was a reporter from the San Diego paper, asking if the fight was in San Diego or Vegas.

It would appear that Joey was looking for protection—both from Pamela Frohreich, the LA district attorney and also from Top Rank, where he recently sold his body.

Joey took a shower and made his phone call for a "deal with the devil." He says he told the agents he was interested and asked what they wanted. They said to call when he got to Vegas.

In the FBI's telling of the same story, Joey, a con man in deep, trying to work a new angle, was untrusting of Top Rank and approached the FBI in their offices, saying, "Just give me a wire, I'll make a case for you."

And in their account, Joey's intriguing and ruthless charm worked again. They told him, "You prove your fight is fixed, and you'll get what you want."

●　　　●　　　●

Joey arrived back in Vegas and got a call from Octavia while he was waiting in the parking lot for his Benz. She asked when he'd be home and told him she was headed to New York. Joey thought she might be a Fed and his paranoia ran rampant. When Joey got home she asked "What's wrong? You look old and stressed."

The phone rang and it was a man with a New York accent, saying that he was Bobby Bennett, and his two friends at the pool in San Diego told him to call Joey. Agent Bennett said, "1 p.m. tomorrow, Gold Coast Hotel, room 319."

The phone rang again and it was Angie. "Hi, honey, where ya been?" Joey had missed their dinner date that Friday. He told her about Scott and claims she said, "That white boy is crazy." Joey wondered if she knew about the FBI. On Joey's voice mail were messages from CNN, David Mattingly, Fox News, CBS, and Oprah doing a story about Eric Davis and Paul Molitor.

There was much to do but Joey could only think about going back to prison and "hustling to stay alive." He fell asleep and awoke to a banging on the door. Feeling naked without a gun, he didn't answer and left out the same door an hour later to meet with the FBI.

Joey arrived at the Gold Coast room and a man answered the door who was about 5'4" and Irish with a New York accent. He introduced himself as Bobby Bennett. He says "The other guy looked like a Mormon with black sunglasses and a square haircut. He was looking out the peep hole and then out the window facing the street. We sat down and they insisted on a tape recorder." Joey says he told them, "Not until I hear the deal and decide that I agree."

Joey claims that Agent Bennett said his supervisor and the Attorney General had spoken to the LA District Attorney and informed her not to challenge Joey's release in return for his cooperation. If Joey signed up to "Clean up Boxing," his state vacated sentence would supposedly not be appealed, and after this operation, Joey would be given a new identity and relocated.

Agent Bennett added, "I have some great news for you, Joey, I spoke to the Attorney General in Washington who met with Senator John McCain, who is monitoring this operation. That's if you are on board Joey?"

Agent Bennett was accompanied by his supervisor Schrump—who informed him that Washington has dubbed this *Operation Matchbook* and Joey's code name would be "Cross."

Bennett informed Joey that he would receive $6,000 plus living expenses for a total of $10,000 each month. They gave Joey some recording devices and a list of boxers they were trying to implicate, including De La Hoya and Foreman. Since Joey had the connections to the Gambino family through his brother, the FBI felt that his entrance into the Top Rank offices would be the key to a major case against them, fixed fights, and Bob Arum.

Joey says he read the contract over and over, as Agent Bennett supposedly informed him, "You will run the show, travel the world, and remember that Senator McCain has spent years trying to get his Boxing Bill Passed, and is aware of you, and will back you".

Joey called Bruce Trampler, knowing that the FBI was listening, saying that he was out of shape and had not entered a ring since prison fights back in 1988. Trampler chuckled and said, "Don't worry about that."

Joey began doing ringside surveillance for the FBI with a recorder in his pocket, capturing Sean's back office conversations.

The FBI found Joey useful but never reliable. He would miss meetings regularly. He was too busy chasing prostitutes, doing coke, and drinking too much Courvoisier. So the FBI decided to get Joey a partner.

Bennett introduced Joey to Agent Harry Schlumpf, a boxing fan from Brooklyn, who said they've been trying to prove Top Rank had been "fixing" fights for years. Joey claims they said "We know your full story. If you can prove that your fight is fixed, you will get what you want. After indictments are served, you will have a new beginning with a new identity."

It was the Buddy Holly-resembling Sean Gibbons that prompted the initial interest of the FBI and John McCain. Between his own fighting career and his matchmaking, Gibbons had drawn a lot of questions about the legality of his methods. Pat O'Grady, the man who trained Gibbons as a matchmaker, was then being remembered for bringing Mexican fighters to the U.S. and then calling immigration after the fights so he wouldn't have to pay them.

In one example, Michael Smith, an Oklahoma fighter with an 0-11 record who was serving a 10-year sentence on a drug-related conviction when the report was released, talked to investigator Skip Nicholson about more than one Gibbons-requested fall in the ring. Mitchell Rose alleged that in 1995 he was offered money by Top Rank to throw a fight against Eric "Butterbean" Esch.

Nicholson's report wound up in the hands of Sen. John McCain, who said its details should be "of significant concern to federal law enforcement authorities" in a two-page letter to then-Attorney General Janet Reno.

The agents were simply the latest effort in trying to make something stick. Schlumpf told Joey, "It will not be easy, you will be wired. We will find you a partner." Joey said his head was swimming as Bobby jumped in, "You'll get paid. Just get Top Rank."

Then Joey claims Agent Schlumpf said, "You owe these people nothing, Mr. Torrey, but we can get you this minute with the Rico Act, for being a known Mafia associate. So get back to us as soon as you make up your mind."

Joey left to drive around The Strip. Pulling into the mall, a fire engine red, SL 320 Benz cut in front of him, into valet parking. He watched a couple get out of the car—a woman in a miniature dress and a small, light-skinned man in a mink coat. The valet told Joey the man's name was Cash and he was a local pimp.

Despite not needing anything, Joey visited Foot Locker when Cash walked up and put his back to Joey. "Where you from, fool?" Cash turned and smiled, responding with, "Inglewood family blood." Joey asked, "Blood! With that fire engine slob mobile?" Joey claims Cash flared and smiled, put out his hand and said, *I saw you on the cover of this morning's paper!*

The two of them began to party together in Vegas. As Cash said, "It's all about the green, all about the money." Cash's wife ran his operation so he could party. Along with Cash's sidekick David Rivera, Joey became part of an outfit resembling the Three Amigos for that year.

Joey was given ringside tickets for a fight at the MGM Grand the following weekend by the people at Top Rank he was currently betraying. Beforehand him and Cash did the Vegas ritual: They hit the mall, nail shop, got facials, dry cleaning, car wash, and waited by the pool until Octavia and Cash's wife arrived.

Sitting in the second row next to Morgan Freeman and Mario Lopez, Mike Tyson walked up to Joey. Morgan Freeman asked who had the rights to Joey's story and Mario Lopez offered to play Joey, but Joey kept wondering what would happen when they found out he was working for the Feds. After the fight, they all went to the after party at Mandalay Bay and the China Club.

That next day Bennett walked up to Joey sitting poolside at the Meridian to tell him they had found someone to be his partner. The 6'1", 310 pound NYC officer Frank Manzione went by "Big Frankie."

The three of them came up with a good back story for Frank Manzione. The undercover veteran had already infiltrated the Genovese crime family, and was so convincing that the mobsters he pinched still had no idea he was the law. Joey saw his thick black hair and shiny silk shirt, and hears an accent out of the hardscrabble neighborhood of Red Hook, Brooklyn. "You look connected," he says. "We should use that."

Joey will introduce Big Frankie as his mob-connected cousin who runs a trucking company back east and wants to get into the fight game. Frank will have plenty of cash and a heavily muscled driver, who is also an agent. The FBI will rent a warehouse protected by razor wire and filled with swag—cases of vodka, racks of clothes, motorcycles, furs—so local thieves will think he's a fence. Big Frankie calls the front YGJ Inc.: "You're Going to Jail."

Joey spent that evening with Sean and Bruce at the office, talking about his schedule. It was the beginning of March and Joey hadn't laced up a glove or run a mile in years, except to the liquor store.

•   •   •

When Joey walked the loser into the blue corner in Corpus Christi, the Bureau had Frankie get his feet wet. They gave Joey a fresh pager that was also a recorder. After inserting a paper clip in a hole, a red light would flash, which meant it was on. He would then say the date and time and then it was good for twelve hours.

Frankie quickly attached himself to and bore into Sean Gibbons, who took a liking to the cop's money and flash. Joey loved that part perhaps the most, but says in private he cried about selling out. With Frankie at his side, there's no restaurant Joey can't crash, no touch too lavish to keep up appearances. When Frankie pulled up to Top Rank in a canary-yellow Porsche, "Nice," was all Joey had to say. With a "cousin" in the mob, Joey found a whole new range of opportunities. He claims, "The FBI wanted me to be a bad guy, so that's the role I played . . . I was buying drugs, ditching cars for insurance money, threatening people."

Joey says that inside himself he felt lost and did a lot of media appearances to fill the time. The family had Joey Cortese, the actor, call him. Cortese and his wife, Kim Delaney, had been trying to sell Joey's story in Hollywood.

At the MGM fight, Joey felt like Big Frankie watched everyone like a Fed. After the fights in Corpus, boxer Jorge Paez was ready to open his mouth about bribes, fixed fights, and more, but the FBI told Joey to hold off.

Trampler had Joey touring the country with Top Rank fights. The ring announcer would introduce Joey, "After 23 years in prison, former A.A.U. champ Joey Torrey will be fighting April 23 at the Anaheim Pond. Tickets available at Top Rank or the night of the fight." Joey would shake both fighters' hands, wave to the crowd, and then go on to the next city.

The next six months were pure pleasure for Joey. "The best time of my life." He stayed at the finest hotels on others' dimes, collecting Polaroids of the prostitutes he slept with while drowning in Bacardi, Viagra, and Vicodin each night. He worked with big-time gamblers to open a strip club together. Joey is feeling so good that he starts planning to buy some land in New Mexico, near Chris Baca's place. He considers resuming his charity work with YDI.

Now with *Operation Matchbook* up and running, Joey isn't worried when he needs to make his next bail appearance that August. He believes the Feds will have his back and never tells his own lawyer, Verna Wefald, about his undercover work—and neither did the FBI. After the judge allows him to remain free, Joey thinks that the parole hearings are just going through the motions and he's out for good.

But Agent Schlumpf began getting tired of Joey's act—the FBI was shelling out thousands of dollars for Joey's cell phone bills, private parties, and routine car crashes. There were embarrassments, like when Joey got drunk wtih Big Frankie at an upscale joint, ripped off his shirt to show off his tattoos and glared at anyone who responded. Joey says that he forgot Frankie was a cop sometimes because Joey felt "happy," which we may as well interpret in this context as "getting paid to drink absurd amounts of alcohol and sleep with prostitutes."

Even getting paid $6,000/month from the FBI, the $4,000 in monthly "expenses," and the $5,000/month Joey received from Top Rank, he was still always broke by the following month, but how long could Joey effectively create tension on and manipulate both parties?

17

The week before his Anaheim fight, Joey moved to the Beverley Hills Hotel. He was bummed, now going to sleep by 2 AM. Where was the endless partying? He claims he flew to Vegas nightly to help Octavia move into their new condo. His days were spent bugging the hotel room in Anaheim for the fight.

Frankie opened up the YGJ warehouse, full of stolen vodka, furs, cars, and paintings. Joey introduced Frankie to Trampler and they hit it off right away. Trampler always needed more financial backing and was looking to open a sports management company. Frankie got so close to Top Rank that they started to ask him to leave Joey at home. Joey describes it as: "The FBI wanted me to go away in the end, as I was more gangster than the gangsters. This was what Frankie and Mr. Sclumpf wanted. They wanted the bad guys to fear me and turn to Frankie for help."

Days before Joey's fight, Frankie, Joey, and the Top Rank crew flew to Texas so Frankie could be introduced to Vern Smith, an associate of Sean's who had fought under nearly fifty different names. Frankie is so enmeshed that *Boxing Digest* later named him the 24th most influential man in boxing. Reality was officially stranger than fiction. Joey was fundamental to the FBI agents gaining enough access to piece together the internal workings of the various deals between Top Rank and its stable of fighters. Like Joey, Frank Manzioni had blended so well into the Top Rank apparatus that he was even offered a job as a cornerman during fights and invited on "scouting missions" for new fighters. Joey knew he was no longer needed by the FBI and he knew how to end it but he was enjoying his $6,000/month plus expenses.

The FBI installed a clock atop Joey's television in the new condo that would begin videotaping when he hit a key chain button. When Smith came to Vegas, Top Rank kept him away from the media and he stayed with Joey. He sat on Joey's couch, detailing every fixed fight he'd been asked to do for Top Rank and asked Joey what round he should go down against Julio Chavez, so Joey could bet on it.

Joey shared the recordings with Frankie who supposedly said, "Washington loves it. We're making history, cleaning up boxing, and Senator McCain is going to get his Presidential Boxing Bill signed based on this investigation." Top Rank seemed to buy the story that Joey and Frankie had the blessing of the family to do business in Vegas.

Then one day Luigi called Joey and asked, "Who the fuck is this Frankie that you're passing off as your cousin?" Joey explained that Frankie was the coke man from the Genovese family and a good friend that you don't want to mess with, meaning that Frankie was not to be questioned about anything and that he was untouchable!

Days before the fight Joey weighed 230 pounds and began to lay off the booze, sticking only to doing coke. During the final days of press, Joey found himself at the MGM Grand where he ran into Emmitt Smith at 2 AM, playing cards alone in the high stakes room. Emmitt waved Joey through his security as he played three hands of blackjack at twenty thousand a hand. They were photographed as Joey thanked him for his support in prison. Joey also observed that everyone from Emmitt to Ana Luisa who had supported him in prison now seemed to be afraid of his wildcard personality.

Meeting in a restaurant with Agent Schlumpf 48 hours before his fight, Bobby Bennett walked in, smiling. Bobby had freshly been reassigned to investigate Furachi and the strip joint Crazy Horse. Supposedly Bennett said that after the fight, Joey could continue working for the FBI on the Furachi case.

•   •   •

The morning of the fight, Joey met the man who bailed him out of prison, Paul Molitor, for the first time at a Denny's in Anaheim. Molitor agreed to continue his favors for Joey and to be in his corner during the match.

Joey then visited Eric Davis. After getting buzzed into his mansion, they sat around while Davis' daughters borrowed the keys to Joey's Benz. Joey asked Eric to be in his corner at the Anaheim Pond along with Molitor. Based on Joey's appearance, Eric asked if he had trained at all. Joey told him, "It don't really matter, Eric. They're fixed anyway."

When Top Rank gave Joey 200 tickets to his fight he claims he passed them out to "every gangster and thug I saw" on 52nd and Hoover; his old stomping grounds.

Bruce Trampler completed a master picture script of Joey's life story, which, presumably was Joey's idea and also at his urging. Ray "Boom Boom" Mancini, a former fighter turned Hollywood producer wanted to make the film. He had been reached through Top Rank's numerous connections. So instead of training for the fight, Joey had a meeting with Avenue Productions about shooting the film.

Allegedly, they couldn't agree if Mario Lopez, Mark Wahlberg, or Jon Seda would be sought after first to play Joey. Eventually they concluded, "Let's wait and see what the outcome is [of the comeback fight], Joey's appeal, etc." Joey thought, "If you only knew that I am taping this meeting and working for the Feds on *Operation Matchbook* to secure my freedom. What a story it is *now*!"

In Joey's hotel room immediately before the fight, Trampler and Sean came into the room; asking Joey how he felt. On the recorded conversation Joey expresses concern about the State Atheletic Commission's test finding his Hep C and disqualifying him from the fight. His Hepatitis is public record in his prison file and has already turned his olive skin to a pale shade of yellow. In Joey's worry he says, "No one is going to let me take this fight." But Gibbons remains calm.

"Don't worry, don't worry," he says. "I'll take the tests for you. Anyway, it's all taken care of. You can't lose."

Joey claims that Trampler produced several blood tests, whiting out names, saying "I have a couple commissioners on the payroll and don't worry about the eye test. I'll take the urine test!"

Joey claims that he was called down to room 430, a hotel suite with the furniture tossed aside. He claims Sean was in there with Perry Williams, whom Bruce Trampler had picked to be Joey's opponent. Williams had been knocked out in the first round of his only previous fight. Joey and the FBI claim Sean had them choreograph the fight in that room, planning each punch and when Williams would go down for the count. Joey claims they practiced it over and over.

Later, Trampler would tell California boxing officials. "I used Williams only because I hoped he would be bad enough for Torres to defeat."

They headed back to the arena for his weigh-in and testing. Joey stripped down, and it was supposed to be the California State Commissioner who checked his fighting weight, but he alleges Sean put him down at 199 lbs. Joey claims that Sean passed an envelope to an old man in a commissioner's suit, and his eye test was passed. Joey also alleges that Sean took the blood and urine test for him.

In the dressing room, while Joey's hands were being taped, numerous celebrities appeared to shake his hand. Top Rank's promotions had created an unbelievable amount of hype that stroked Joey's ego.

The announcer began, "After these messages, the remarkable story of Joey Torres." Joey put on his trunks—minutes away from his first professional fight. On the night of April 27, 2002, at 42 years old, Joey finally got the chance he'd dreamed of all those years in prison. Davis and Molitor walked in with Trampler as the live K-Cal 9 TV crew followed him through the tunnel.

Top Rank sells a heart-wrenching version of Joey-approved events: A promising young boxer fell prey to gangs and drugs, was arrested for a murder he didn't commit, plea bargained for five years in juvie to avoid a life sentence, and just days before his release, a judge sent him to a state pen for 25-to-life. From there, this underdog helped kids on drugs and uncovered an obscure law that got him out after 23 years. Next we are treated to Carlos Palomino, who confirms Joey's talent, and Eric Davis, who testifies to his good heart. It's a solid and convincing tale.

Joey walked out of his dressing room and through the velvet curtain wearing a robe embroidered with the words, "Thug Life." The arena was packed with 5,000 fans, but they reportedly laughed when he disrobed to display his 5'6" frame at 230 pounds. The media began speculating that Top Rank's hype about Joey's gym dedication was just that.

The music began with, "Baby, I'm a Thug," and people were grabbing at Joey and snapping photos. Eric and Molitor held the ropes open as he stepped in. The announcer repeated Joey's story as "the comeback kid." Joey claims the announcer had tears running down his face but ESPN says it was Joey who was crying. As the announcer rang the bell twice, he finished, "After 22 years in prison, Joey Torres refused to accept [his judicial fate], studied law, and found a way out—always thinking of that one fight he always wanted! And tonight is the night!"

Joey's first punch missed badly but Williams' first right hand sent Torres down, face first onto the canvas. Joey says he only remembers the fans going crazy, Octavia crying, and the bell ringing as he is looking up from the canvas, with one glove under his ass as the referee countied in slow motion, "one...two...." Joey claims he looked at Arum, who was sitting in the front row saying, "Ohhhh, nooooooo," and the arena went dead quiet. Joey stumbled up at nine, looked at the referees holding his gloves, sure he was going to stop the fight. Joey claims that Williams punch hurt more than anything he'd experience previously in life. Perhaps it was the lack of cocaine.

At 1:05 of the first round, a glancing blow to the left side sent Williams down, only to fall again after he gets up from a slow-motion hit to the same spot.

"You have to wonder if Williams wants to fight at all," the announcer ponders out loud as the bell rings.

Joey wasn't acting like a pro fighter and was missing the choreography he'd supposedly been trained on. Despite this, Joey was called to the middle of the ring and managed to hold his opponent for the next full two minutes of the first round. Instead of going after the crippled Torrey, Williams put his gloves in front of his face and barely threw another punch that round. As bad as Williams looked, Joey looked worse.

Joey was sent out again in the second round. Thirty-nine seconds in, after a series of lunging punches, Joey threw his left, his opponent falls and stays down. Everyone was booed for their bad acting jobs, as the throng of spectators chanted "Bullshit! Bullshit!"

In the post-match interview, when Joey is asked if Williams gave an honest effort, he leans toward the mic to say: "I hit him with good body shots. People don't know what a good body shot can do . . . No matter what anyone says, I made it. I made it."

But the crowd isn't buying it and in the resulting melee, 16 people who were furious about the seemingly fixed fight were arrested and Torres was hustled out of the arena while protesting that it was clean. The media called Joey both flaccid and overweight. Both fighters were suspended for their lack of ability.

Joey had an after party with his crew and some strangers. He drank his liquor but still hurt from that first round punch. He now feels he should never have been in the ring with Hep C, his vision, and after gaining eighty pounds since his last fight. Back in Vegas, Frankie notified Joey that Washington loved the fight.

"He wasn't really serious about [the fight]," said former U.S. Olympic world champion coach Kenny Adams, who helped Joey train. "Joey only trained four or five days at the most. The only reason I worked with him during that time is he said he may be in a movie and that I could work with him in the movie."

Afterwards, Arum was still eager to help Joey (though he later referred to it as a "favor"), who became a fixture around Arum's Top Rank offices.

"I'm a believer in him," Arum said at the time. "He comes out of prison with a burning desire to do things for others."

Pamela Frohreich seethed at the "I-didn't-do-it" spin that Joey and Top Rank put on his murder rap, as she felt he expressed no remorse. She didn't care that Joey was working for the FBI, which she only learned about in a call from the Vegas U.S. attorney's office in late 2002. The FBI didn't seem to care anymore either, who reportedly told her through a federal prosecutor, "Keep us informed, but don't do Joey any favors on our account."

On his birthday, May 4, 2002, Joey was tired and regretted getting involved in all this. He was alone, working for the FBI, fearing that his worst fears were coming true.

18

In July, Joey is in Gibbons' office when a boxer has dropped out of a match against Billy Zumbrun, a heavyweight Top Rank is pushing up the ranks. "You want it?" Sean offers Joey. "Nah," he replies. "I'm in worse shape than before." So Gibbons offers it to one of his best losers, 34-year-old Brad Rone.

A gap-toothed, 259-pounder with 25 sequential defeats—Brad Rone lost to Zumbrun just three weeks prior. He's been barred from fighting in Nevada. Rone still accepts the $800 and the fight with under a week's notice. His mom dies that week but he still sticks with it. Joey and Sean are partying one night in Vegas when they hear that Rone literally had a heart attack and died in the ring.

Questions begin to surface about Rone, and Joey suspects that time is short for Top Rank.

Nine months since Joey first walked into an FBI office in San Diego, he has delivered on fixed fights and got Frankie inside Top Rank. While the FBI is grateful, they want him out of the picture now. In December Joey announces his intention to see Costa Rica and Schlumpf tells him, "Go. Stay as long as you want. We'll make sure you get your checks."

Joey packed a bag for Costa Rica and stopped in Managua to visit Alexis Arguello at his gym. Joey gave him a hug and thanked him for his support. Having new stabbing liver pains, Joey increased his medication and bought a villa a block from the beach in Costa Rica. He thought surfing might start to heal his body from all of the drugs and Hepatitis.

On May 19, 2003, Joey flew back to LA to hear Frohreich argue against the vacated verdict. His tanned skin in an Armani suit sat in the back row of a hearing room at the ornate Court of Appeals. Joey was sure that the situation was fixed and they were just going through the motions; that Joey would be pleading to time served, but his lawyer, Verna Wefald, was outgunned. Frohreich and two other prosecutors are hammering away, and the judge is listening: Didn't Torres appeal his sentence 20 years ago? Why should he get a second chance?

Joey shifts in his seat nervously. He sure didn't expect this. "You can never tell," Wefald tries to reassure him when the hearing ends.

Wefald wrote a letter to the DA, and told Joey that she was trying to close a deal on him pleading to manslaughter and time served. She argued that Santana had made a deal and lied on the stand to put Joey away. Joey wanted to return to Jaco, where his only concern was working on his tan.

Joey jumps in a rental car and drives back to Vegas, where he finds Frankie at The Meridian pool. "You gotta help me, Frankie. I'm in real trouble here." he says. Hoodwinking Joey as he did upper management at Top Rank, Frankie says, "I'll see what I can do." Joey pleaded with Agent Schlumpf to call Senator McCain's office and tell them to back off Top Rank. The continued investigation was only going to take away the one thing he had left—matchmaking and ringsiding.

In Vegas, the FBI, Top Rank, and everyone else was on the warpath. Joey walked into Top Rank and was met by Sean at the door who walked him downstairs saying, "Senator McCain is calling for an uncut version of your fight. The world's media is saying it was fixed. Have you read the paper?"

Joey hadn't. They sat in Sean's car as he supposedly keyed some coke. Sean allegedly apologized for Williams knocking Joey down, that Top Rank hadn't "used" him before and it wouldn't again. Joey got a call from Trampler, who demanded, "Tell Sean to get upstairs now."

Joey called his attorney who said, "I just had an interesting visit from a man who said that he is your cousin Frankie, from Brooklyn, and he wanted to know if there was anything he could do to help in your case."

Joey went by their apartment and found Octavia talking on the phone. She hung up as Joey walked in, sarcastically announcing, "That was Ana. What a great wife you have." She packed her things and that was the last Joey saw of her.

Four days later, Joey's worst fears were confirmed: "The trial court is directed to reinstate [the] defendant's first-degree guilty plea ... and the sentence of 25 years to life." Wefald tries to insist it's not over. She has discovered evidence that Santana, Joey's chief accuser, was also a suspect, which wasn't revealed at his trial. She convinces the court to allow her client to stay out on bail while she prepares his appeal, but everyone knows that the clock is ticking.

Knowing the FBI no longer wanted him to hang around Vegas, Joey switched it up and began working as muscle for Top Rank. Joey says he flew out to New York and was told to go into Cha Cha's Pizzeria, a mob joint he claimed Trampler had connections to, and begin infiltrating their operation. Joey carried an envelope with $5,000 in cash and a pistol. He says he always carried a gun because he didn't like how the FBI carried themselves and figured he'd eventually need it. A limo dropped off Joey in front of Cha Cha's, where he says he saw agents across the street. Joey sat in the back of the restaurant, waiting for Cha Cha and said the date and time into his recorder.

Cha Cha walked in and Joey says he told him about Furachi being squeezed and how Trampler had suggested they talk. Cha Cha counted the money and said, "*Grazie*. I will make some calls." With that done, Joey returned back to the hotel, gave Schlumpf the recorder, and blew off some steam.

Joey met with the FBI prior to meeting with Trampler, who wanted to take him for a drive. Joey was fairly sure that this meant Trampler knew he was working for the FBI and it was all over, but they just went down to the Orleans Casino to see Trampler's friend Tony Danza, performing a one man show. Trampler asked Joey about New York but Joey says he seemed to know the whole story from Cha Cha already.

Trampler went with Joey to his next bail hearing to work on the movie script about Joey's life. There was still no plead out option being offered. They had lunch with Boom Boom Mancini and Ed O'Neil. Trampler supposedly went on and on about fixing all of Boom Boom's fights on Joey's recorder.

Joey thought that Trampler—known for being a savant and a genius—could see right through him. Trampler always talked about how he hated rats. On the way back to Vegas, Trampler told Joey about a family friend, Dino DaVinci, who owned one of the nation's biggest off shore betting establishments in Costa Rica, and he would make the call for Joey. Frankie was in so deep with Sean and the drug dealers—that he brought in another agent to play his girlfriend. Joey visited Angie, who was concerned and sensed that something was not right. He picked up an envelope after hours to be delivered to DaVinci and left on a red eye for Costa Rica.

He met DaVinci at the twenty story building that he claimed housed Sportsbet.com and 2bet.com. Trampler claimed to Joey that they bring in a million dollars each week. The competition across the street was supposedly being run by Jimmy Sacco. Dino was waiting for Joey.

One night at the El Rey Casino, Joey claims he saw Bonnano and his crew, who invited him over. Bonnano supposedly ran bets and wanted to know what it would take for DaVinci to go away. Joey says he played stupid, like he didn't hear him and walked out.

Joey received a call from Trampler, who told him that Oscar De La Hoya wanted to meet with him so Joey flew back and they headed to Big Bear, CA, where Oscar was training for his Yory Boy fight.

Joey told Trampler about DaVinci and the murder for hire. "Dino is a good man from the Rhode Island family that I know from the boxing scene. What you do is your business." Joey claims Trampler told him. Joey returned to Jaco and claims he sat Dino down and told him about the green light with a $50,000 tag, but that he was willing to hear other offers.

The following week, Dino's courier was hit for six figures coming out of the bank. Someone in his own family was a traitor who had stolen ledgers valued in the millions. Dino left town, selling the last of his company to Jimmy Sacco.

Joey talked to Frankie who told him that there was a problem with some guy named Rodriguez threatening Top Rank's managers if they didn't use his fighters. Joey only knew one Rodriguez, and he was not a "made" guy from the Mexican mafia, but an associate! Frankie supposedly said, "That's the guy!"

Frankie and Joey walked into Top Rank's offices and met with Trampler, Cameron Dick Dunkin, and another manager, who was being squeezed by Frank Rodriguez. Frank asked Top Rank, "What do you want done?" Joey was chosen to threaten

Rodriguez at the Anaheim Pond. Frankie called in Avi, another agent, to be added muscle.

Joey and Cash arrived in Anaheim and were put up in suites by Top Rank. They left their guns in the room and didn't tell anyone they were there. There was a knock at the door, and when they asked who it was, Frankie responded, "FBI." Cash apparently didn't take him seroiusly, as he laughed for the next few minutes.

That evening, as the fights were going on, Joey and Cash walked into the arena and saw Trampler, Frankie, and Avi sitting near the velvet curtain leading into the tunnel. Joey and Cash sat down and made eye contact with the trio. In the ring were the two boxers, with Rodriguez in the red corner. When it was all over and Rodriguez started walking back through the curtain, Joey fell in behind him with Cash at his heels, startling Rodriguez. Joey supposedly asked, "Mr. Rodriguez, could I have a minute of your time?" Rodriguez turned and recognized Joey and saw Cash with his hand under his jacket. He smiled. "Sure," keeping his back against the wall. Joey informed him, "You are not mob. I am. You are not shit and a minute away from getting taken out. You do not threaten Top Rank fighters, managers, or janitors. For good faith, you are going to sign over your fighter Salido to my cousin Frankie and Cameron Dunkin, right?" Cash tapped his arm to signal that security was walking up, and they split.

Joey claims they again ran into a shaken Rodriguez as they were leaving the arena, fumbling with his car keys. Joey claims he put a gun in Rodriguez's mouth and the following day, the U.S. Gov't owned a lightweight boxer named Salido.

•   •   •

Joey returned from yet another bail hearing with his attorney when he says Big Frankie did not sound like himself and supposedly told him "You better talk to your attorney. I think the FBI is going to screw you. Washington is being told shit about this. They do not understand being exposed on the streets like we do."

Joey still felt sure that he would not go back to prison. He had been paid over a quarter million dollars by the FBI. He had delivered countless recordings and other evidence. He was about to take a week off to check out property in Albuqerque and reconnect with Chris Baca and YDI. He met with Baca and accepted a job, figuring this would be his home when it was all over, his ego figured he wouldn't need witness protection because he was "the only true gangster Top Rank ever knew."

Still collecting $6k per month from the FBI and $5k more from Top Rank for muscle and promotions, Joey sold a 6 month option for his movie rights for another $50k and started designing boxing gear for urban kids. Life seemed almost too good to be true. Joey was so confident that he did not even use any of this money to hire a better attorney and continued working with the public defender.

He traded in his Benz for a Jeep Wrangler and went to see Verna in LA. She said the DA would not accept their deal, and it did not look good for Joey. For the previous week, the FBI was not taking his calls, and Frankie said, "Let's see what happens at the hearing." Joey stood numb when the Judge declared, "Denied. The order of December 19, 2001, granting the petition for coram nobis is denied and guilty plea reversed, and the defendant is re-sentenced for 25 years to life imposed."

Joey gets in his jeep and heads to visit a girlfriend in St. Louis, then continues, purchasing a ticket to Mexico to "go swimming with the dolphins in Cozumel." But on Sept. 14, the clock runs out; his motion for a new trial is denied. Joey was supposed to be in LA to turn himself in two days later. Arriving at the Vegas airport, he looks for his connection. Then he sees a flight to Costa Rica and thinks "Screw it," and heads to Central America.

Joey's logic was that the DA needed him to have a case. If they send him back to prison, the FBI will have to present the audio tapes and contracts and admit they had a deal with him. It's bad for Joey either way. He wanted to tell Verna about the FBI but was too ashamed. In hindsight, he figures he could have worked with her to secure his freedom.

Yet another girlfriend, Pamela, picked him up at the airport in Costa Rica. Joey told her that while things didn't look good for him, the FBI owed him $50,000, and they could build a life together in tropical paradise—surfing, tanning, knowing there was nowhere on earth to run. So Joey kept calling Frankie for his money, who said he was talking to people. Joey figured if he was sent back to prison, he was a dead man for sure.

But at this point Schlumpf and Big Frankie had no allegiance left to Joey and were trying to help track him down to return him to prison. They fed his periodic requests for money to various law enforcement agencies hunting him down. *He's in Costa Rica. He's in Mexico. He's in Panama.*

In late October, Schlumpf and Frankie are in Washington, reviewing *Operation Matchbook* with their superiors, when they hear that Joey is back in Vegas. They fly back, but he is gone by the time they arrive.

Joey had met with Trampler, not knowing if or when Bruce would know about the FBI and when the raids would begin. Trampler was aware of what happened in the court of appeals as he was speaking to Verna daily, trying to save Joey from going back to prison. Joey claims they schemed about a place to hide him but nothing came to mind.

It seemed only a matter of time before the world would know that Joey had double-crossed Top Rank. Joey fled to Tijuana, where he sold his rental car and claims he walked off with a backpack, gun, $5,000, and a change of clothes. Joey spent the next two months of his 601 days of freedom on a Mexican bus from Mazatlan to Chiapas to Mexico City. His his passport had been revoked.

Not knowing what to do and continuing to trust the FBI, Joey called Agent Schlumpf, and they agreed to meet at the Mirage Hotel. Joey feared it might be a setup and took a few shots of tequila before crossing the border from Tijuana.

Joey expected to be shot in the back at any moment, having betrayed so many former allies. In classic Joey form, he blamed the FBI for his isolation. The only person he could think to tell about his FBI deal was Chris Baca but felt too ashamed in the end. Joey says he left his gun in a giant flower pot and took a taxi to Henderson's Grass Valley Inn in Vegas. He went back to feeling the only safe place for him would be protective custody and that he had to trust the FBI.

Joey claims that Trampler continued to send him money daily, still not knowing about his betrayal.

Joey called Ken Hurdle, from the Department of Corrections as he drove up to the casino to meet Frankie. Joey told Ken everything over the course of an hour. Ken tried calling the FBI, Frankie, and his handler, hearing stories of violence, havoc, and other horrors. Joey decided to skip the meeting with Frankie and Ken promised to be in the court room and make sure that DOC put Joey out of state until the matter was cleared.

Finally, in December, someone tipped off the Vegas police that Joey was in town to see Angie. He was sitting in his room at the Four Queens Hotel when the phone rings. Joey picks it up, but no one is there. A minute later, the door to his room exploded as a task force of FBI, Metro, ATF, and U.S. Marshalls point their guns at his head, laid him out on the floor, and carried him away. "Tell the FBI, 'thanks for burning me,'" Joey screams.

His bail revoked and returned to court, Joey spent Thanksgiving in the Las Vegas County Jail. Joey again called Ken Hurdle and Agent Schlumpf, asking to be put in protective custody.

•   •   •

Joey was put in the TV day room of LA County Jail. A kid reading the paper looked up at him. He saw someone move to his right, then felt a pain in his neck. Joey pushed his way out of the room as the blood ran down. Joey fell and pulled a pencil from his neck.

He was put into segregation but not allowed placement into protective custody because the LA County Jail sheriff couldn't confirm his story with the FBI about his claims of assistance in *Operation Matchbook*. Joey stopped showing up for his media interviews, fearing each was a setup.

Joey was taken to Norwalk Superior Court where he stood in the holding tank awaiting escort to the court room. Bailiff Rick appeared, shaking his head. Joey looked up at Judge Knupp, who was also shaking his head. Krupp sentenced Joey to life in prison and gave him credit for his 24 years served. He was released to California DOC.

Joey arrived in Kern County where a lot had changed. He was treated like a new inmate with a new number and put in maximum security with a parole consideration of 2065. Joey wrote daily to Ken Hurdle, utilizing his prolific jailhouse hustling skills. Joey was sent to Mule Creek State Prison,

Sensitive Needs Yard—not because of the FBI investigation and his undercover work, but because of his prior protective custody needs for saving the life of the female correctional officer.

To date, the California DOC has not complied with Joey's requests to be moved out of state or into witness protection. Because he was attacked, Lieutenant Rendon and Captain Dave Arnold eventually investigated his claims but he remains in California.

•   •   •

A month after Joey went back to prison, the Feds pulled the plug on *Operation Matchbook* and on January 6, 2004, sixteen FBI agents raided Arum's office, removing computers, medical records, fight tapes, boxer contracts, and financial documents.

The warrant named Trampler, matchmaker Pete Susens, manager/agent Cameron Dunkin, and Sean Gibbons, who was fired later that month for reasons unspecified. Sean's history of being investigated prior to his employment at Top Rank came to light as well as how he had come to be known the "Oklahoma Meat Packer."

When the *Las Vegas Sun* asked Oklahoma Department of Labor commissioner Brenda Reneau Wynn to elaborate on the allegations about Gibbons she emphatically said "Ugh."

Boxing columnist Katherine Dunn wrote: "Oklahoma state boxing regulators reported that an Oklahoma meat packer named Sean Gibbons ... ran a revolving stable of bad-to-mediocre boxers who traveled the Midwest pretending to fight each other under phony names, creating fraudulent wins for fictitious fighters with 'respectable' records."

While it was difficult to prove many of the charges, it appeared that Sean had a history of bringing in bribed fighters to lose multiple times, fighting under multiple aliasses to bolster the rank of fighters he was trying to promote. Compounding the charges alleging that he would bring in fighters from Mexico, were those accusing him of calling in the border guards to send them home without pay.

Investigator Skip Nicholson's 26 page report alleges that Sean had "boxers using at least one other alias (sometimes three) and Social Security number, fraud, forgery and fight fixing."

Arum, who personally had risked the most to help Torrey with huge amounts of cash and offering him his first professional fight well into middle age, finally became bitter when he understood that the man he had gone out of his way to help had conned and betrayed him, but he still did not comment and kept his PR staff mostly silent on the matter.

A spokesman for Top Rank did say the company "does not know the scope of the government's investigation" but intended to continue "lawfully co-operating with it".

In a scene befitting of virtually everyone's perspective and behavior in this scenario, Arum's friend Bill Caplan paints Top Rank as the victim: "That's all [Joey] was. He was a con artist," said Caplan, a fight publicist. "Bob just wanted to give the guy a break. He paid thousands in expenses for him, knowing he would never make anything. He was just trying to give him a chance at having a new life."

Based on Frank Manzoni's reports that he compiled with Joey's help, police are now investigating allegations of fighters taking the ring under multiple aliases, soft match-ups to assist popular boxers and widespread "skimming" of fighters' fees by Top Rank executives. De La Hoya and Esch fights were both put under scrutiny amid suspicions that—quite unknown to either of them—their opponents were bribed to be beaten.

Even in Las Vegas, a city built on a history of crime, the citizens were transfixed by the story of one of the most colourful police operations in the city's history.

19

Joey says that the most common question he is asked is "What was the best experience in your two years of freedom?" Contrary to what you might expect from a man who endlessly partied on the FBI's dime till the wee hours of the morning with cocaine and prostitutes, he claims it was "seeing the world at a lower level from hostel to hostel, bus to bus, and his final month in Mexico and South America." And perhaps that's true. Perhaps all of the excess was just his expression, yearning for something missing in his life.

Eligible for parole since 1994, Joey has become increasingly bitter about his extended sentence and lack of prospects.

And to this day he waffles back and forth between the mantra he repeated through B.A.D. and YDI, *"reject the easy path of victimhood."* and, well, does exactly that, claiming that he is the victim of the FBI, the judicial system, the mob, and even the street gangs. He says "The decisions that you make today can and will matter in years to come, so why blame it on bullshit and stop being a victim."

But yet, as recently as 2012, as Joey watched three inmates be taken to the Parole Board for release, he again paints himself as the victim.

Joey describes the situation as: "It was not the parole board that freed those men: No, it was that those inmates had family and money to be able to 'pay' for there loved one to be freed!" One of the men was denied for five years. He had no representation and was serving life for 3 strikes after being caught with one gram of cocaine.

The other two had committed grisly crimes. One had served 15 years on a rape and murder, and another 18 years for killing his own daughter. They were all released.

In the same wind, Joey blames his lack of family, his lack of representation, and his lack of cash as the reasons he hasn't been freed. It's as if he hasn't read the clear legal briefs about why Pamela Frohrenrich went after him so fervently for so many years—that his lack of remorse, his distortion of the truth, and, yes, his twisting of the details of each situation to make himself appear as the victim.

Joey fails to accept that the DA sees remorse in these men. Instead, he'll give you an extended speech about how unfair it is that a good lawyer costs good money and how freedom shouldn't have a price. While we can all more or less agree to that as a rough and moral concept, the particulars are where it gets nasty.

There are things that we may never know. Did Joey walk into the FBI office in San Diego and offer dirt on Top Rank, thinking that it would assist him in his parole hearings? There doesn't seem to be any reason why the FBI would lie about this detail.

We may never know if the man Joey murdered was his crooked boxing manager withholding money from him, but his perspective differed notably from the stories that his friends told. While I'm sure that many reading this far can relate to what it's like to be a painfully bored teenager longing for a more interesting life, it can never justify the crimes that Joey does admit to, even if you accept that his home life was less harmonious than it would appear on paper.

•   •   •

Like clock work, Joey receives numerous letters from attorneys vowing to have him paroled for five to ten thousand dollars. He was appointed the great Tracy Lum, Esquire who informed him that it was a good time to be released, but without his pals at the FBI or Top Rank, Joey no longer receives monthly checks of $5,000-10,000 and can't change how he spent each of them on a month of partying.

On May 29, 2009 Joey was scheduled for another parole board hearing. He was 100% sure that this time he would be released and that "justice" would prevail.

As Joey walked into the parole board room that hot May day, he sensed that something was wrong. As Joey was seated he saw an elderly man with a gold shirt and green pants nudge down his glasses and state, "I don't care who you were or who you are, this is gonna be a fair hearing." *Yeah, right,* Joey thought, smiling, and said, "Good morning to you too sir."

These are the transcripts from that May 2009 appeals court hearing:

```
 1   living in society being the best person I could be.  I
 2   thought that you would say I'm going to go see the
 3   governor's aide and try to --
 4         PRESIDING COMMISSIONER ANDERSON:  Let me tell you
 5   this, sir --
 6         INMATE TORREY:  Sincerely, Sir, with all due
 7   respect I mean this from my heart --
 8         PRESIDING COMMISSIONER ANDERSON:  Let me tell you
 9   this, you had a chance to talk.
10         INMATE TORREY:  Yes, Sir, I know.
11         PRESIDING COMMISSIONER ANDERSON:  Now it's my
12   chance.
13         INMATE TORREY:  Yes, Sir.
14         PRESIDING COMMISSIONER ANDERSON:  Okay.  Now, let
15   me tell you this.  It's not about you.  It's about the
16   State of California.  This is not about your ego and all
17   the things you've done.  We recognize those things you've
18   done and we've read them.  This is not about you.  You
19   are no different than anybody else.  You have complied
20   with what the rules are in CDCR.  The rules say you have
21   to program.  You don't get any special privileges.
22   Nobody does.
23         INMATE TORREY:  I've been the best I can be, Sir.
24         PRESIDING COMMISSIONER ANDERSON:  But I'm saying
25   JOSEPH TORREY     V-21699     DECISION PAGE 11   5/29/09
```

```
1    and here's a problem for you, sir, that you need to work
2    on. Your start date is 2004. Okay. Now, here's the
3    issue, should you receive a grant our charts allow us to
4    calculate the grant from when the lifetime starts. They
5    have the life term starting in 1/23/2004. So now you do
6    a grant and post-conviction credits, you have no post-
7    conviction credits prior to 2004. So in essence whenever
8    you do get a grant, and I'm sure you will get one if you
9    keep following the rules and the recommendations of the
10   Board, you get four months a year of post-conviction
11   credits. The Board does not go back and look at prior
12   post-conviction credits. We go from the date of when the
13   life term starts. So you got a 25-year commitment and
14   you get a grant there is no provisions right now to give
15   you post-conviction credits back to your original start
16   time. That's a problem. You need to work on that. I
17   don't know how you're going to do it.
18        INMATE TORREY: As in my BPT report, I'm amazed
19   how saving this officer's life and being free for two
20   years didn't even come out of either one of you. I'm
21   amazed. I'm mind boggled how I suffer everyday getting
22   beaten and saving her life and it's just goes in the
23   wind. I'm amazed how being free for two years -- I got
24   denied for two years, the same two years I was free and
```

If you've read this far, you know that Joey's start date was long before 2004, but a "misunderstanding" like this is not something an inmate serving a life sentence can easily correct without an expensive attorney.

Joey's state-appointed attorney explained to the commissioner that Joey had served his time and the only reason Joey was appearing in front of him was based on being eligible for parole.

Joey's attorney stated: "I will leave a record for 'our appeal,' and I will get you free." Joey again thought freedom would be right around the corner.

At first Joey says he was told that he would be released if he could obtain his credits for time served. So he wrote the parole board office in Sacramento explaining this error, but it remained uncorrected.

Joey says he maintained faith in Attorney Lum; she appeared to be in his corner. After about a week Joey got called to pickup his legal mail. It included the following letter from Tracy Lum, requesting $5,500:

Tracy Renee Lum
Attorney at Law
6680 Alhambra Avenue, #214
Martinez, California 94553-6105

Telephone 925.387.0607   trlum@hotmail.com   Fax 925.387.0500

Joseph Torrey, C.D.C # V-21699
Mule Creek State Prison, B10-150L
P.O. BOX 409040
Ione, California 95640-9040

Dear Mr. Torrey,

The decision by the Board of Parole Hearings in May of 2009 to deny your parole and to give you a two-year denial was absurd. The fact that you were not given credit for twenty-four plus years in custody is more than difficult to deal with. **In spite of this, the fight is not over!** The Judge who re-sentenced you to prison after your co-operation with law enforcement and successful parole period said, *"Torrey get something in front of me if you are not paroled."* Mr. Torrey you need to file a Writ of Habeas Corpus and ask a Court of law to consider reviewing the injustices in your case.

My fees regarding Writs of Habeas Corpus include **a flat fee of $5,500 for the three State Courts.** This fee is non-refundable even if the case is won at the first level of Court. There is an additional flat fee of **$5,500 if you want to proceed to the Federal Level of Courts** if your case is unsuccessful in State Court. I'm willing to continue the fight on your behalf. Although there are no guarantees, I believe your case could be successful if brought to the Court's attention and I hope you can raise the funds to move forward.

Until the final bell (as you would say),

Tracy Lum

Tracy Renee Lum
Attorney at Law

Unable to afford Tracy Lum, Joey thought his best chance would be Judge Espinoza's Democrat and pro-inmate views, as well as his "letter of the law" approach.

In October 2010, Joey was called back to the legal mail desk. He felt that he had articulated the appeal properly and presented the facts. Joey took a deep breath and read:

SUPERIOR COURT OF CALIFORNIA, COUNTY OF LOS ANGELES

DEPT 100

Date:	OCTOBER 12, 2010			
Honorable:	PETER ESPINOZA	Judge	J. A. RAMIREZ	Deputy Clerk
	NONE	Bailiff	NONE	Reporter

(Parties and Counsel checked if present)

BH006298
In re,
JOEY TORREY,
Petitioner,
On Habeas Corpus

Counsel for Respondent:

Nature of Proceedings: ORDER RE: PETITION FOR WRIT OF HABEAS CORPUS

The Court has read and considered the Petition for Writ of Habeas Corpus filed on August 18, 2009 by the Petitioner, the Return filed on July 14, 2010 by the Respondent, the supplemental letter filed on July 23, 2010 by the Respondent and the Traverse filed on September 14, 2010 by the Petitioner. The Petition challenges the Board of Parole Hearings' (Board) May 29, 2009 finding that the Petitioner was not suitable for parole and denying him parole for two years. The Petition also challenges the Board's calculation of the Petitioner's time credits and minimum eligible parole date, as well as the California Department of Corrections and Rehabilitation's failure to merge his prisoner files.

The Petitioner was initially received into the Department of Corrections on February 6, 1980 after he was convicted of first degree murder and sentenced to a term of 25 years to life in prison. See Petition Exhibit C, pg. 4. He was then ordered released on January 9, 2002 after he prevailed on a writ of error corum nobis regarding his plea agreement. See Petition Exhibit D, pg. 1; Petition Exhibit E, pgs. 13-14; Petition Exhibit H. That order was reversed and the Petitioner was returned to custody on January 23, 2004. See Petition Exhibit F, pg. 1. During the 2009 suitability hearing, the Board indicated that the Petitioner would not be afforded credit for any time served prior to 2004 and that his minimum eligible parole date was January 23, 2004. The Board also found the Petitioner unsuitable for parole, denying him parole for two years. See 2009 Board Hearing Transcript, pgs. 72-88.

Subsequently, the Petitioner's time credits and minimum eligible parole date were corrected to reflect the time he served prior to his release in 2002. He is now being given credit for serving his sentence between February 6, 1980 and January 4, 2002 and from January 23, 2004. See July 22, 2010 Letter From Respondent, Exhibits A and C. Additionally, due to the Board's errors, the Petitioner has been scheduled for a rehearing on November 19, 2010. See July 22, 2010 Letter From Respondent, Exhibit B.

The Court finds the Petition is moot, because the changes requested by the Petition have been made and he has been granted a new suitability hearing in light of those changes. Although Petitioner remains in custody, the only remedy available to him from his Petition is for the Court to grant it, directing the Board to reconsider Petitioner's parole suitability in accordance with due process. See In re Rosenkrantz (2002) 29 Cal.4th 616, 658. Because a rehearing has already been scheduled, the Petition is moot. See In re Holmes, (1989) 214 Cal.App.3d 483, 484. Should the Board determine that the Petitioner is not suitable for parole at the rehearing, the Petitioner may then contest the legitimacy of his continued confinement with a new Petition.

1

Minutes Entered
10-12-10
County Clerk

Joey received a modification order and Philip Reisner, Chief of Legal Affairs, articulated the errors that he had corrected, but Joey needed the California Department of Corrections Legal Affairs to correct the mistake of giving him a new prison number and processing him as a new inmate.

Joey sent a complaint to the Judge in LA.

Board of Parole Hearings   State of California

MISCELLANEOUS DECISIONS

FACTS

Joey Torrey, V-21699, was denied parole for two years on May 29, 2009. Torrey was originally committed to CDCR on a life sentence for first degree murder in 1982. In 2002, he was released on an appeal bond and recommitted in 2004.

When he returned to CDCR in 2004, he was treated as a new commitment and given a new CDC number (old number was C-47754), new MEPD, and a new classification score.   C-47554

Torrey's CDC records under his old CDC number were not consolidated into his Central File under his new CDC number. In reviewing the May 29, 2009 hearing transcript, it appears that the panel may not have had access to certain records, under his old CDC number, that would be relevant to a determination of his parole suitability.

CDCR institutional staff are in the process of merging his records and recalculating his MEPD and classification score.

RECOMMENDATION(S)

Schedule Torrey for a new hearing on the next available calendar.

STAFF (Name) Philip Reiser	TITLE Staff Counsel	DATE 7/14/2010

DECISION(S)

Schedule Torrey for a new hearing on the next available calendar.

VIA U.S. MAIL

Subject: CONTINUED INCOMPETENCE

Mr. Reiser:

    I do hope that this missive finds you well. Per your BPT 1135 dated July 14, 2010 (Miscellaneous Decisions, see attached), I was assured as I attended my Board of Prison Hearing on November 19, 2010, that your department's continued blunders had been corrected. A blunder that caused me seven (7) years of unfair and prejudicial CDCR decisions and board hearings. But on November 19, 2010, I was astonished to be informed, prior to even entering into the BPH room by my attorney Jay Dyer, that I was being postponed pending a new "Psychological Report."

    How can I be denied my freedom again based on more blunders by your office? Shouldn't your office have ordered, "Need New Psychological Report?" And if not, why wasn't it? How can you, as legal counsel, continue to be harmfully misguiding and misinforming after signing your name to an order for a new hearing? I am amazed and would truly like to know how this can transpire after my previous hearing in 2008 was postponed for the same reason, and incompetence ran wild there as well. I was informed then that I did not need a new report. (see attached). And at my 2009 BPH hearing I was bamboozled as the only thing that Commissioner Anderson requested of me was to obtain thirty (30) years of earned credits via the court; but there was no mention of needing a "New Psychological Report"!!

    I was sure that Judge Peter Espinoza, the Deputy Attorney General Jennifer L. Heinisch, and your office of "Legal Counsel" had this injustice corrected; and per due process, I would be entitled to a fair and impartial hearing. I can only hope that you have the class and professionalism to respond to this justified inquiry - This is my life.

Receiving a stack of legal letters in reply, Joey learned he was rescheduled for another parole board suitability hearing on February 3, 2011.

Joey took his medication with a hot cup of tea and looked out through his window that is the size of a carton of cigarettes. He saw a bird fly by and in his head it signified that he would accept whatever decisions came his way and would pursue peace and calm.

On April 7, 2011, while listening to Amy Winehouse's *Love is a Losing Game* eleven times, Joey wrote a letter to commissioner Anderson which he made 50 copies. He began mailing a new copy to Anderson every few days.

Joey says for awhile every day felt closer to freedom.

But then a new man walked into Joey's cell. He hit Joey's right eye, then delivered a hook, then connected a head-butt. Joey claims he broke his old typewriter over the man's head, ending the fight. While adrenaline was pumping and he was in survival mode, Joey says he stepped over the body, put a book in the hinge so they would not be locked in the cell together, dragged the man into the shower, kicked him in the teeth, and walked back to his cell with a cut and swollen face.

Joey was pissed to lose his typewriter but says he could not report the incident, for a write up of any infraction deemed to be his fault would result in another five year denial from the parole board.

Days later, Joey saw the same man in the yard talking to himself and eating grass. He found out a week later that the man ran in on him because Joey had refused to give him a cup of coffee and that others were eating Joey's discarded trash before him.

Joey claims he did not remember this guy but does find it amazing how much other inmates clamor for his apple cores and rotting food. He does remember that once an inmate brought him a *Sports Illustrated* magazine he had tossed the day before, trying to exchange it for a cup of coffee.

•　　　•　　　•

Joey stood at the door, awaiting an interview with his counselors, wondering what they could want. Prison counselors can prevent a transfer or other such complications.

Joey entered and Counselor Bond, a rough, old school Marine freshly back from Iraq, stated that he would be writing Joey's updated parole board report and was given permission to sit in on the parole board hearing. The counselor urged Joey to obtain "parole plans."

The state needed to know that Joey had a residence and a job awaiting him. Joey explained that everyone in his family was dead and asked how he could obtain parole plans from inside. Who would send a letter stating they'd hire a convicted murderer serving *life* upon release? How do you find a new residence from a cell?

Joey called Katie Alsobrook, a new friend that he'd begun writing and talking to on the phone. She offered to help him in any way she could. Joey got back in touch with Sister Sean from the Catholic church in Los Angeles. He had sent her drawings to sell at church fundraisers and in return she offered to provide him with a place to stay if he could come up with $500.

• • •

The way the parole system works, a convict is released right back to the same locality from which they were living before arrest. So convicts with a background of gangs or drugs, or who are simply marked for death, are released into the same streets where the same elements are waiting for them, often into their old habits. When someone in trouble is released from prison back to their old neighborhood, there are almost always hundreds of people waiting, eager to kill them. If a released convict flees the county, they are marked as "fugitive on the run and parole violator."

State officials endure enough bureaucracy that they rarely address this reality and their interests remain in parole violations and, as a result, creating a system of recidivism.

Joey fears that even if he found a way out, anyone who remembers him from saving a prison guard or working with the FBI might see to making a quick end of him.

• • •

Four months later, Joey obtained the credits needed for parole. He wrote to Commissioner Anderson informing him of this but not did receive a response. Joey wrote a second time and to officers who had helped him over the years. Joey was informed by Counselor Bond that he needed to obtain some "Laudatory" chronos, or what we might call letters of support.

2049 South Santa Fe Avenue • Los Angeles, CA 90021-2819 • Phone 213-438-4820

March 22, 2010

Board of Parole Hearings Desk
Mule Creek State Prison
P.O. Box 409099
Ione, CA 95640

Support Letter
Not Confidential

Re: Joey Torrey – #V21699

Dear Board of Parole Hearings Members,

My letter affirms Joey Torrey in his release back into the community. Mr. Torrey has served thirty-years in prison. He has used his incarcerated years well to grow into maturity, sensitivity, improve himself educationally and to expand his marketable skills. Mr. Torrey is an excellent artist with exceptional talent. Likewise, it would not be an exaggeration to say that the way in which he has used his talents to help at-risk youths is extraordinary. Joey's involvement and presence in programs such as Boxers Against Drugs (BAD) and New Mexico's Youth Development Inc (YDI) have given at risk youths an example of hope and change. Mr. Torrey's dedication to helping others is remarkable.

Through the Partnership for Re-Entry Program, we support Mr. Torrey in housing at Francisco Home - 40th:
     1224 W. 40th Place, Los Angeles, CA 90037.
Or at Francisco Home – Leighton:
     1135 Leighton Ave, Los Angeles, CA 90037.
The first location houses eight persons and the second up to fourteen people. Both are transitional living homes for men that are close to public transportation and within a couple of blocks of each other. Residents are required to attend house meetings weekly, which include a Bible study and an AA meeting. If it is necessary, Francisco Home will support Mr. Torrey in attending additional regular AA or NA meetings in the neighborhood. We ask for $100 deposit and $500 monthly rent, adjustable according to employment. We work with each individual to assure that financial resources are not a limitation for their housing. Availability of room is assured, but the location at either home will be determined at the time of release.

I also offer a position in the Office of Restorative Justice when he is released. The position is for clerk in the Partnership for Re-Entry Program (PREP), a mentoring program that supports parolees upon release. This is a volunteer position to help with the transition. The position would include filing, letter writing, phone calls, computer work, and generally supporting us in our work to reintegrate parolees into society. Additionally, PREP works in partnership with Ernest Roberts at PVJobs [www.pvjobs.org] and guarantees Mr. Torrey an interview with Juan Alvarado, job developer, upon release. Mr. Torrey has learned marketable skills that will enable him to enter the job field. PREP will support Mr. Torrey until he secures a job and affirms him in his return to society through the community of Los Angeles.

Mr. Torrey's years of detention have given him a new perspective of life and a desire to be a conscientious, law-abiding and self-sufficient citizen of the community. He has taken his rehabilitation seriously and has proven this by his active involvement in BAD, YDI and countless other at-risk youth organizations. Surely the prophet Isaiah speaks to the justice system when he says: **"Comfort, O comfort my people, says the Lord. Speak tenderly to Jerusalem. . . he has served his term"**. I implore you consider finding Mr. Joey Torrey suitable for parole release when he appears before you.

I remain,

Sister Mary Sean Hodges, OP
Director, Partnership for Re-Entry Program, PREP
213-438-4820 ext. 23

cc: Mr. Joey Torrey
    CCI Bond

NAME and NUMBER: **TORREY, JOEY, C-47554 or V-21699 (B10-150L)**   CDC-128-B (Rev. 4/74)

Recommend that Inmate Torrey be considered for release on his next available Board of Prison Hearing (BPH). I met I/M Torrey at CTF-Central over twenty years ago when his CDCR # was C47554. I/M Torrey has always been truthful, respectful and acted with the utmost integrity when interacting with staff. In 2004, we again crossed paths at MCSP, where I was the CCII Supervisor on Facility B.

When Torrey and I were on B Facility at MCSP, Torrey had just been returned to prison from a release on an appeal bond. Many things had been happening that were detrimental to Torrey's period of incarceration. These things included his being issued another number (V21699) which also resulted in the deletion of the previous twenty-plus years he had already served. On numerous occasions, I sat with Torrey to encourage him to maintain his positive attitude, to stay on course and to not lose hope that he would prevail. Torrey always maintained his positive attitude, educated himself and kept insight into his crime, all the while patiently waiting for the system to catch up to the situation.

Two events that stand out with Mr. Torrey that attest to his character and rehabilitation:

1. In 1982, he saved a correctional officer at CMF from being beaten and raped by another inmate, despite the retribution that was eventually taken against him. Torrey has always addressed the issue as "doing what was right" indicating that he had at least gained enough insight into his crime that he understood what the responsible thing to do was and he eventually suffered an assault by the inmate that attacked that officer.

2. While released on an appeal bond, Torrey was free to do as he chose, without parole or any other supervision. Torrey did not receive so much as a parking ticket in the two years he was out of prison. He was also living in Costa Rica at the time he was ordered back to prison. Instead of ignoring the order and remaining in Costa Rica, he returned and faced his peers and accepted responsibility for his actions.

In closing, Torrey has served his sentence with the utmost honor and integrity. He has conducted himself as all people should and has been an inspiration to other inmates as to how they need to conduct themselves. Mr. Torrey has great respect from his fellow inmates and staff. Rehabilitation is a key component when determining which inmate qualifies for release. Based on his years of incarceration coupled with all of his accomplishments that he has earned as a programming inmate, Mr. Torrey deserves another chance at being a productive citizen. Recommend he get this chance.

Original C-file
cc: Writer
       Inmate

D. ARNOLD
Correctional Administrator
California Medical Facility

LAUDATORY CHRONO

DATE: 7-19-2010   CALIFORNIA MEDICAL   GENERAL CHRONO
                                      FACILITY

Joey was again called to legal mail from the loud speaker and was handed a letter from Vacaville, checked the name, and opened it while walking across the yard back to his cell block. Joey slowed his gait as he read, to the point that he claims he was standing in the middle of the yard while a soccer game was going on, with people yelling at him.

Counselor Bond had informed the old Captain Dave Arnold about Joey's case, and his lack of parole. Captain Arnold was now Warden Arnold and violated the unwritten rule of state administrators—he went to bat for an inmate. Arnold felt he saw a change in the Joey he had known as his inmate to the one who had saved his officer.

•   •   •

Joey was appointed yet another State Attorney who visited him, sure that he would be paroled; but then supposedly requested $5,000 to "truly put [Joey] over the top," or for $10,000, represent Joey in all levels of appeal when denied.

On February 2, 2011 Joey sat outside the hearing room as the sun set on the window behind the commissioner. He had to wait as yelling ensued between the Commissioner and other inmates for almost two hours, but finally it was Joey's turn and he entered the gloomy room with green name plates in front of each member.

He said everyone smiled except for Commissioner Gilliam, who instructed him, "Son be seated, what do you want?" Joey stated his name and what he expected to happen.

Commissioner Gilliam then turned to Joey's attorney and stated, "I have been here since 7:45 a.m. and Joey wants to hurry this up?" Joey burst out, "Bitch, I've been here since 1979, and I demand a fair shake!"

The Commissioner explained that Joey was being denied his freedom based on a history of violence and breaking the rules. Joey had received an Advisement of Expectations report for refusing to take a Tests of Adult Basic Education (TABE) test in 2004, claiming he had already taken one in 1979. Joey has since received his GED and Associate of Arts Degree.

The 76 year old Commissioner's voice rasped like that of a smoker, as she compared Joey to the previous inmate. Joey's state attorney then said, "Mr. Ramirez, has served his time!" Commissioner Gilliam replied, "Maybe if you got his name right and filed the 236-D Form he would be going home." His parole was denied.

The commissioner asked Joey if he had anything to say. Joey stated, "Respectfully, Ma'am, Commissioner, how can I be considered a threat when I was released for two years, traveling the world and never committed not even a traffic ticket?" [sic]

Continuing to plead with the commissioner, Joey stated, "I was free for two years and every time my car went past 55 mph, I slowed thinking of this day, and how I was to turn myself in on 01/24/2004, and how proud you all would be of me, an old time lifer released after serving 25 years and returned." Did Joey rewritte history that he'd turned himself in?

Without missing a beat, the Commissioner responded, "Unfortunately you were released, but I am going to solve this right now because I'm tired, Parole denied until November 2013.

The hearing had gone by without a mention of him saving the officer from being raped or his 20 years without a serious infraction of the rules, other then refusing to take a TABE test. He now claims that the reason he did not take the TABE test is because they had identified him based on his old CDC number and that supposedly the instructors had told him only to appear for his current CDC number.

In a few months the Commissioner retired, forcing Joey to wait three more years for his next parole hearing.

California Board of Parole Hearings
Arthur Anderson, Presiding Commissioner
Post Office Box 4036
Sacramento, California
95812-4036

Subject: PETITION REVIEW

Dear Mr. Anderson;

I do hope that this missive finds you well. I wish to begin sorting out my hearing conundrum beginning with my May 1, 2008 hearing that was a confusing calamity with the presiding Commissioner stating, **"There's something wrong here."** (See attached "A"). The Department of Corrections failed to clear up this blunder; and I am again brought in front of you Commisioner Anderson on May 29, 2009. You tell me that I need to get credits for decades served and points made properly applicable. (See exhibit "B"). I then spend the next year in the law library getting all that you requested through a writ of Habeas Corpus, the courts corrected what the Department of Corrections refused to correct; while simultaneously I wrote the Board of Parole Hearings hoping that someone would correct this error (See exhibit "C" & "D" hereto).

Following this I was assured by your legal affairs division that a new hearing would be held as soon as possible. I was sure justice would prevail after complying with your directive and including two (2) years free in society, that would equate to my being paroled. (See exhibit "E"). Sir, I was assured by you and your associates, on and off the record, that this continued blunder and 'bum rush' would end once I was given the credits that you requested.

On November 11, 2010, I was inspired that I'd be paroled with all credits made applicable, but I was utterly astonished when the attorney John Dyer informed me prior to walking into the hearing that my hearing was going to be postponed again. He stated, after leaving Commissioner Arbaugh, "Good news is you are going to get a date, Bad news is they are postponing this hearing till you get a new Psychological report." (See exhibit "F"). Heart in hand I was amazed that the BPH and CDC&R would of, and should of, known prior to this hearing that I needed this new Mental Health report; and once again was sure that on my new scheduled date February 2, 2011, justice would prevail!

Commissioner Anderson, I did _everything_ that you asked of me to obtain my parole. <u>Everything</u> and more that has been asked of me. And sadly when I walked into the parole board hearing I was verbally disrespected by Commissioner Gilliam, and to this day 'still' do not know why I was denied parole <u>but again</u>?

Commissioner Anderson, you looked in my eyes and gave me your word that if I did what you asked, all would be just fine. I have now served 33 years on a five (5) year plea agreement. I have watched kids parole who have half my time on much more brutal and heinous crimes. Commissioner Anderson you told me what to get corrected... And through my effort the court gave me back my old CDC&R number (C-47554), something that the Department of Corrections refused to do.

The courts stepped in and did what no one else would. Lets be honest Commissioner Anderson, I would not have been scheduled for a parole hearing in May of 2009 if I was not eligible right? I did what I was forced to do, burdening the courts. I am only a man who has been the best that he can be. The problem is that you request something, then I do not see you again? If you please take the time to read the attached Exhibit "F", you will see that <u>Hearing Comments</u> state: "the inmate's attorney has prepared for this hearing and has requested to represent inmate at his next scheduled hearing." Point in case sir, I was given a new attorney and <u>never</u> saw these Board Commissioners. This wasn't intentional, was it? Re-stacking the deck against me?

Respectfully, Commissioner Arthur Anderson, from one hearing to another I am informed to complete a task; then denied after completing what was requested of me. Therefore I am requesting a new, full and "fair" hearing; during the 'day time' and not at 8:00 p.m.; as in my last hearing. Because, all I recall is Commisioner Gilliam stating how tired she was and to hurry it up.

In closing, I thank you for your valuable time on this critical (freedom) matter. I can only hope that you will do what is fair Commissioner Arthur Anderson. I have completed <u>everything</u> that was requested of me on May 29, 2009; and, to this date completed <u>every</u> task and, leaped through every hoop; I rightfully deserve a Petition review granted and new hearing forthwith...please.

Respectfully submitted,

Joey Torrey
C-47554 : B10-150L
MCSP : POB 409040
Ione, California
95640-9040

CC: Legal Petition
    Legal Affairs
    K. Alsobrook
    A. Bond, CCI
    T. Lum, Esq.
    G. Cruise

On June 1, 2012, Joey watched other life inmates released on parole who had served half the time that he had. One kid had not even been born when Joey arrived in prison, yet had served 15 years of a life sentence. Each of them had attorneys.

Joey says he spent many years pondering how he could raise $10,000 for a qualified attorney as there was no one to give or loan him the money. Though he did demand it from me over a period of months, but unfortunately, I do not have $10,000 either.

Joey wondered what became of his celebrity friends and why he hadn't heard from them. He remembers having $10,000 dinner bills during his extravagent years in Vegas.

In July Joey was again called for legal mail line and received the following letters:

STATE OF CALIFORNIA --- DEPARTMENT OF CORRECTIONS AND REHABILITATION   ARNOLD SCHWARZENEGGER, GOVERNOR

BOARD OF PAROLE HEARINGS
P.O. BOX 4036
SACRAMENTO, CA 95812-4036

August 13, 2009

Joseph Torrey
V-21699 B-10-150L
Mule Creek State Prison
P.O. Box 409040
Ione, CA 95640-9040

Dear Mr. Torrey:

This is in response to your letter received by the Board of Parole Hearings (Board) on April 29, 2009. Specifically, you requested that the Board's hearing panel take into consideration releasing you on parole at your May 29, 2009, parole consideration hearing.

Unfortunately, the Board was not able to respond to your letter before your May 29, 2009, parole consideration hearing at which you received a two (2) year denial. Your next parole consideration hearing is due in May 2011. At your hearing you were given the opportunity to discuss your issues and/or concerns.

Sincerely,

ELIZABETH OHLENDORF
Staff Services Manager II
Administrative Division

Joey believes the problem is that he refuses to tell the parole board what they "want" to hear. On August 2011, after his last appeal was denied, based on a mental health evaluation, Joey was summoned for a parole board mental health report, and found to be A-1 except for being a narcissist. He says he did not know what it meant to be a narcissist.

Joey, long known for his detective skills, seemed perhaps unwilling to learn or acknowledge they were referring to his selfishness, vanity, pride, and ego—his attitude of *I do what's best for me in any given scenario and then attempt to justify it later*.

UnCommon Law

220 4th Street, Suite 103
Oakland, CA 94607
Tel: (510) 271-0310
Fax: (510) 271-0101
www.theuncommonlaw.com

Keith Wattley
Managing Attorney

July 12, 2012

LEGAL MAIL
Joey Torrey (C-47554)
Mule Creek State Prison
P.O. Box 409040
Ione, CA 95640

Dear Mr. Torrey:

We are sorry to hear of your recent denial from the Board of Parole Hearings. Unfortunately, we do not have the resources to represent clients without a fee. Our fee to file a writ challenging the BPH's denial is $10,000 for all three levels of state court (Superior Court, Court of Appeal, California Supreme Court). Half the fee is due up front, with the balance due 60 days after the petition is filed. If that fee does not work for you, we could charge $3,500 to draft the petition for you and ask the court to appoint us. In that case, the full amount is due up front.

The only way to get a hearing sooner than 3 years is if you petition the Board through a Petition to Advance Hearing (1045a form). Lifers can use a 1045a form to request an earlier hearing if they can show some new information or changed circumstances that make the longer denial (in your case seven years) no longer necessary or reasonable. If you would like us to file a 1045a for you, our fee is $2,000.

If the fee is acceptable to you, please let us know and we will send you a fee agreement that explains what our representation would look like. Please also send us a copy of your parole hearing transcript when you receive it. Thank you again for writing, and we look forward to hearing from you again soon.

Sincerely,

Ritika Aggarwal

Ritika Aggarwal
Paralegal

The person performing the exam was a short, attractive, 20-something woman. She asked Joey to sit down and then asked if he ever thought about killing himself and why he did not participate in the "A.A." program. Joey complained to her about listening to child molesters blaming their mothers for not loving them and how he needed a drink.

She smiled and asked Joey what he felt about himself. Joey told her that in order to make it this long in a cell, locked for 23 hours a day, not knowing when or if the next man wants to kill him, that in order to survive, he "must" think "that the sun rises on my ass, and sets on my crotch."

She asked Joey if he was a narcissist. He says he smiled and asked her why she wears make up, lip stick, and plays with her hair. Joey says "If my only crime after 35 years is that I think awesome [sic] about myself, then wow, the system is truly broken." While he's quick to contradict himself to claim he was "out there in society obeying all the rules and speed limits," he seems to actually believe this despite what he wrote of that same time in his own memoir less than five years prior. He's quick to ignore the parts of the story that condemn him and reacts angrily when someone suggests that his story contradicts itself. He doesn't seem to notice that this is exactly why the State of California is so insistent on holding him while they release people convicted of far more grevious crimes (who also generally happen to hire attorneys that costs in the tens of thousands of dollars).

•   •   •

Unshakeable, Joey finds a new girlfriend who he dubs "Queen Meshelle." She mails him articles including one about Senator McCain and his "Boxing Bill." Joey sat for an hour looking at this document and reading the date and noticing that he is still being mentioned eight years later in June 2012.

STATEMENT BY SENATOR JOHN McCAIN INTRODUCING THE PROFESSIONAL BOXING AMENDMENTS ACT OF 2012

June 18, 2012

Washington, D.C. – U.S. Senator John McCain (R-AZ) today delivered the following statement on the floor of the U.S. Senate introducing the Professional Boxing Amendments Act of 2012:

"Mr. President, today I am pleased to be joined by Senator Reid of Nevada to introduce the Professional Boxing Amendments Act of 2012. This legislation is virtually identical to a measure reported by the Commerce Committee during the 111th Congress, after being approved unanimously by the Senate in 2005. Simply put, this bill would better protect professional boxing from the fraud, corruption, and ineffective regulation that has plagued the sport for too many years, and that has devastated physically and financially many of our nation's professional boxers.

"My involvement with boxing stretches back a long way – first as a fan in my youth, then posting a painfully undistinguished record as a boxer at the United States Naval Academy, and then over my time here in Congress, where I have been involved in legislation related to boxing since the mid-1990s.

"The 19th century sportswriter Pierce Egan called boxing the 'sweet science,' while longtime boxing reporter Jimmy Cannon called it the 'red light district of sports.' In truth, it's both. I have always believed that at its best, professional boxing is a riveting and honorable contest of courageous and highly-skilled athletes. Unfortunately, the last few decades of boxing history has – through countless examples of conflicts of interest, improper financial arrangements and inadequate or nonexistent oversight – led most to believe that Cannon's words best describe the state of boxing today.

"The most recent controversy surrounding the Pacquiao-Bradley fight is the latest example of the legitimate distrust boxing fans have for the integrity of the sport. After the Pacquiao-Bradley decision was announced, fans were clearly apoplectic and many commentators found the decision astonishing.

"Bob Arum, the longtime promoter representing both Pacquiao and Bradley, said: 'What the hell were these people watching? ... How can you watch a sport where you don't see any motive for any malfeasance and yet come up with a result like we came up with tonight. How do you explain it to anybody? ... Something like this is so outlandish, it's a death knell for the sport.'

"ESPN boxing analyst Dan Rafael – who scored the fight 119-109 for Pacquiao – called the decision an 'absolute absurdity,' saying, 'I could watch the fight 1,000 times and not find seven rounds to give to Timothy Bradley.'

"Additionally, following the fight, HBO's Max Kellerman was ringside where he said, 'This is baffling, punch stat had Pacquiao landing many more punches, landing at a higher connect percentage, landing more power punches. Ringside, virtually every reporter had Pacquiao winning by a wide margin ... I can't understand how Bradley gets this decision. There were times in that fight where I felt a little bit embarrassed for Bradley.'

"Clearly, the conspiracy theories and speculation surrounding the fight are given life because there are so many questions surrounding the integrity of the sport and how it is managed in multiple jurisdictions. Professional boxing remains the only major sport in the United States that does not have a strong, centralized association, league, or other regulatory body to establish and enforce uniform rules and practices. Because a powerful few benefit greatly from the current system of patchwork compliance and enforcement of Federal boxing law, a national self-regulating organization – though preferable to Federal government oversight – is not a realistic option.

"Ineffective oversight of professional boxing will continue to result in scandals, controversies, unethical practices, a lack trust in the integrity of judged outcomes and most tragic of all, unnecessary deaths in the sport. These problems have led many in professional boxing to conclude that the only solution is an effective and accountable Federal boxing commission.

"This legislation would establish the United States Boxing Commission ('USBC' or Commission), providing the much-needed oversight to ensure integrity within the profession through better reporting and disclosure, requiring that the sport avoid the conflicts of interest which cause fans to question the outcome of bouts which hurts the sport. If enacted, the Commission would administer Federal boxing law and coordinate with other Federal regulatory agencies to ensure that this law is enforced; oversee all professional boxing matches in the United States; and work with the boxing industry and local commissions to improve the safety, integrity, and professionalism of professional boxing in the United States. More specifically, this legislation would require that all referees and judges participating in a championship or a professional bout lasting 10 rounds or more be fully registered and licensed by the Commission. Further, while a sanctioning organization could provide a list of judges and referees deemed qualified, only the boxing Commission will appoint the judges and referees participating in these matches.

"Additionally, the USBC would license boxers, promoters, managers, and sanctioning organizations. The Commission would have the authority to revoke such a license for violations of federal boxing law, to stop unethical or illegal conduct, to protect the health and safety of a boxer, or if the revocation is otherwise in the public interest.

"Mr. President, the Professional Boxing Amendments Act would strengthen existing federal boxing law by improving the basic health and safety standards for professional boxers, establishing a centralized medical registry to be used by local commissions to protect boxers, reducing the arbitrary practices of sanctioning organizations, and enhancing the uniformity and basic standards for professional boxing contracts. Most importantly, this legislation would establish a Federal regulatory entity to oversee professional boxing and set basic uniform standards for certain aspects of the sport.

"Thankfully, current law has already improved some aspects of the state of professional boxing. However, like me, many others remain concerned the sport continues to be at serious risk. In 2003, the Government Accountability Office (GAO) spent more than six months studying ten of the country's busiest state and tribal boxing commissions. Government auditors found that many of these commissions do not comply with Federal boxing law, and that there is a disturbing lack of enforcement by both Federal and State officials.

"Mr. President, it is important to state clearly and plainly for the record that the purpose of the Commission created by this bill is not to interfere with the daily operations of State and tribal boxing commissions. Instead, it would work in consultation with local commissions, and it would only exercise its authority when reasonable grounds exist for such intervention. In fact, this bill states explicitly that it would not prohibit any boxing commission from exercising any of its powers, duties, or functions with respect to the regulation or supervision of professional boxing to the extent no consistent with the provisions of Federal boxing law.

"Finally, with respect to costs associated with this legislation. The price tag for this legislation should not fall on the shoulders of the American taxpayer, especially during a time of crushing debt and deficits. As such, to cover the costs, the bill authorizes the Commission to assess fees on promoters, sanctioning organizations and boxers; ensuring that boxers pay the smallest portion of what is in fact collected.

"Let there be no doubt, however, of the very basic and pressing need in professional boxing for a Federal boxing commission. The establishment of the USBC would address that need. The problems that have plagued the sport of professional boxing for many years continue to undermine the credibility of the sport in the eyes of the public and – more importantly – compromise the safety of boxers. This bill provides an effective approach to curbing these problems. I urge my colleagues to support this legislation."

A year earlier Joey had learned that Senator McCain had to return "gifts" that he had received from Bob Arum, the same man that he vowed to convict for fixed fights. So after learning of this, "Cross" got back in touch with his old friend and hopeful benefactor:

SUBJECT : "Operation Matchbook - Fixed Prize Fights"

Honorable Senator McCain:

My name is Joey Torrey, and in 2002 I took part in a "Fixed Prize Fight" which was held in Anaheim, California. Approved and sanctioned by the U.S. Attorney General's Office and caught on audio and visual surveillance administered by the FBI an calle "Operation Matchbook." I spearheaded this operation under the code name of "CROSS." The aforementioned fight was so blatantly fixed that the following day as I sat in Top Rank's Office your staff, Senator called for a copy of my fixed fight on video.

Subsequently, after serving 25-years in a California Prison my sentence was vacated I was then released in 2002, and received a phone call from Bob Arum of Top Rank wh had remembered me from the 70's when I was a stand out amateur boxer. Mr. Arum made the opportunity to exploit my time served and forged a 'come back' promotion. I the flew to Las Vegas to meet Mr. Arum and explained that I was 42 years old! Mr. Arum smiled and stated, "Kid, you just show up and your opponent will fall when told." I signed a contract and then went down the hall to meet with a great man, Sig Rogich of Rogich Communication, who told me not to trust Arum. I returned back to my hotel and thought that I did the right thing when I called FBI Special Agent Bennet and told him my story, asking him, "What should I do?"

One week later I met with Agent Bennet, who informed me that if I signed on board t "clean up boxing" that my criminal appeal by the state would not be challenged, and I would remain free. I was then informed that you Senator were abreast and planned to name your Bill after me. I did all that was asked of me in allegiance with the greater cause of cleaning up the sport that I love. Yet, this very day I am back in this prison cell serving a life sentence (again!) <u>with no new crime having been committed!</u> And on my return to prison in 2004, was informed that Mr. Arum made "Operation Matchbook," and myself, disappear. I have enclosed an article where you mention the operation yourself. Yet, I sit with no umbrella of protection from you, nor the FBI. I have even attempted to obtain my contract which is being held from m under FOIA. I am now sure that you must not be aware what the FBI did to me or the operation Senator McCain.

In closing, I sincerely thank you for your valuable time and consideration on this matter, literally, of life and death. I pray, and await your response with 'hope' that you will demand the bell of justice to be heard and launch an investigation. Do peruse the enclosed <u>FACTS</u>; possibly view me via YouTube@ The Joey Torrey Story. But whichever way that the winds may blow Senator, you <u>must</u> establish a "U.S. Boxin Commission!" No child or future champ should ever enter the ring of 'hope' only to exit broken and bamboozled by the nihilistic Bob Arum's of the sport. Do stay stron Senator, and always keep your left up.

Until The Final Bell,

Joey Torrey

But Senator McCain tried to continue to bury and forget about the failed "Boxing Bill."

JOHN McCAIN
ARIZONA

COMMITTEE ON ARMED SERVICES
COMMITTEE ON HEALTH,
EDUCATION, LABOR, AND PENSIONS
COMMITTEE ON HOMELAND SECURITY
AND GOVERNMENTAL AFFAIRS
COMMITTEE ON INDIAN AFFAIRS

United States Senate

241 RUSSELL SENATE OFFICE BUILDING
WASHINGTON, DC 20510-0303
(202) 224-2235

2201 EAST CAMELBACK ROAD
SUITE 115
PHOENIX, AZ 85016
(602) 952-2410

122 NORTH CORTEZ STREET
SUITE 108
PRESCOTT, AZ 86301
(928) 445-0833

407 WEST CONGRESS STREET
SUITE 103
TUCSON, AZ 85701
(520) 670-6334

TELEPHONE FOR HEARING IMPAIRED
(602) 952-0170

October 19, 2012

Joey Torrey
C-47554: B10-15OL
MCSP: POB 409040
Ione, California 95640

Dear Joey:

Thank you for contacting me regarding the launching of an investigation. I would very much like to be of assistance.

However, it is the customary practice of the U.S. Senate to allow a Senator from the constituent's home state to assist him or her. Therefore, I have forwarded your correspondence to Senator Dianne Feinstein. I am confident that she will provide you with the appropriate assistance.

Again, thank you for contacting me. I hope your situation can be favorably resolved.

Sincerely,

John McCain

John McCain
United States Senator

When Bradley's fight appeared to be fixed in October, 2012, Joey, *Operation Matchbook*, and the Boxing Bill each appeared in another news cycle, but Joey remains in his cell serving his new life sentence with no help on the horizon.

Joey alternates between blaming Senator McCain and the FBI for his extended stay in prison after the supposed promises of eternal freedom. Perhaps things could have gone differently if Joey had been more of a team player.

It didn't help the prosecution that Arum had connections with the Attorney General's Office, that he fired Sean Gibbons promptly, and that no one with any evidence against him could talk without implicating themselves at the same time.

But Joey has burned many bridges, some of them repeatedly, but new people still get in touch periodically, offering to help.

Joey continues to push for McCain, as chairman of the Ethics committee, to request his contract be made public record for the purposes of his defense, launch an investigation, and have Governor Brown pardon him.

And again Joey recuses himself from all blame, saying, "I am told to do something about it, but what can I do but tell this story and back it with the facts?"

•　　　•　　　•

Between the side effects of his medication and a failed attempt to replace his knee, Joey says he had become deeply depressed from 2009 until recently. His health has been in decline and his weight had decreased from 230 to 190 pounds by September of 2012. His new friend Katie pushed him to go see the doctor and eat right. She began mailing him food and milk thistle for his liver, but these kind of relationships have never been long lasting in Joey's life. Will he see freedom before his downward spiral finishes him or some other hazard of prison claims his life?

"If the police ask for help, just say no! If the FBI comes knockin, do not answer the door! When you read, 'Former Boxer Joey Torrey has died,' you can remember, 'Oh snap. I just read his story.' I am amazed and saddened that since this return to prison in 2003, not one so-called friend has written to me. I am entering my 35th year of incarceration. To be abandoned after all I have done for so many is crushing. I always thought friends surround and protect you. I did sell my soul to the devil, but I saved the life of a woman being assaulted and clothed many a child. If anything I regret, it's signing my soul to the devil for the promise of freedom... I will be assassinated by the hand of someone you read about in this story. Thank you for your time. Stay true. Stay strong. "The fault, dear Brutus, is not in our stars, but in ourselves..."

—Joey Torrey, 2007

(EPILOGUE)

Before I completed my research, I assumed, based on what he had written to me in letters, that Joey's life was the product of never having a proper grounding at home in his formative years. So it gave me pause when I learned he was the product of affluence. At the same time, the suburbs can be the most desolate place of all and having a high-powered executive for a father—especially when you yearn for street cred—can be the loneliest place, lacking support. Still, it's not so easy to conclude what went wrong.

As a teenager with a half-dozen arrests, including one for assault with a deadly weapon, a probation officer wrote that Joey "demonstrated an ability to play both ends against the middle. He's personable, likable and bright, but ... almost a pathological liar." Joey's ability to convince an almost unbelievable number of people of his variations on numerous events speaks excellently of his charisma but alarmingly of his morality.

To this day Eric Davis says, "He was cool. He never lied to me."

While the public pressure campaign from celebrities and professional athletes seemed to help Joey briefly escape his life in prison, it was those same stretchings of the truth that enraged Pamela Frohreich to seeing that Joey's altered perception of events would ensure that he spends the rest of his life behind bars, or at least until his perspective shifts to understand things in a way that aren't always flattering to himself.

Joey Torrey is undeniably a leader figure. And leaders, like lawyers, his other natural inclination, tend to have narcissistic traits. According to Michael Maccoby, author of *The Productive Narcissist,* the productive ones learn to retain an element of their egos while moderating the negative side effects of narcissism. According to Maccoby, the leading traits are:

- Enjoying leading others and telling them what to do.
- Being an entertainer
- Generally young and male
- Being an impatient, compulsive workaholic
- Frequent lies to make yourself seem better
- Dressing better than other people, regarded as attractive
- Liking to swear
- Waiting for other people to stop talking before you start
- Putting your needs before others
- Engaging in a lot of sexual hookups
- Cheating in relationships
- Feeling no remorse about the people you hurt
- Being dumped after four months of dating someone
- Hating being criticized
- Finding ways to punish others when you feel rejected
- Seeking admiration by devaluing others.
- Parents that were ignoring and adoring simultanesouly
- Choosing male friends to attain a higher social status
- Dropping names during a conversation to feel important
- Excessively bragging about having a perfect family

Other than the last point, which seems debatable, it's not surprising that the parole board's psychologist saw a model narcissist in Joey. Seeing his frequent contradictions, how he handled himself on the outside, and how he talks about those matters now, it articulates in one word what motivated Pamela Frohreich to go on her crusade after him.

For Big Frankie Manzioni, despite his cover being blown, *Operation Matchbook* was an unqualified success, but for Joey, all of the outrageous parties eventually had to have a morning after. Now he's a known police informer and was again transferred to Mule Creek State Prison, on the property near Soledad.

Frohreich said: "It's tempting to think a guy has done 20 years and it's time to let him go," Frohreich said. "But the more I saw, the more I felt he wasn't rehabilitated."

Frohreich talked to investigators who worked the case, went over old reports, and interviewed witnesses. She concluded Torres' story of wrestling a gun away from his former manager and accidentally shooting him was just that—a good story. So she convinced a court to reject Torres' bid for a new trial.

Similar to his gang involvement, it's impossible to know if Torrey and his brother were actually involved with the Italian mob and organized crime, or if this was another good story.

Even after Joey ran away to hide in Mexico to avoid going back to prison, the friends he'd made through the phone lines understood and sympathized with his behavior.

"Let's say you've been locked up for 24 years, would you want to go back?" Davis asked.

Asked if he regrets having fled, Torres shrugs. "You gotta understand, I was scared. I didn't think I could do another day." But he has—ten more years. He still calls the two years spent with the FBI "the most beautiful time of my life."

"Right now my brother's a sitting duck," said Marcy Bautista, his sister. "The other inmates think he's a rat, an informant."

•　　•　　•

In his dressing room before his big televised fight, Joey says he thought about those who were no longer in his life—Sonya, JoJo, Ana Luisa, his parents, Emma, Dolly, and Blanca, but perhaps his analysis lacked the perspective to show how it was his own actions that pushed each person away.

After finding out that he was working for the FBI, Smith, Molitor, and Davis eventually stopped returning his calls or those of reporters seeking comment about their long-standing ties. As a girlfriend who asked that her name not be used explains: "You have to understand. He burned a lot of us."

Meanwhile, Senator John McCain continues to push for the Professional Boxing Amendments Act. The bill, which would protect fighters by strengthening safety measures and monitoring medical histories, passed the Senate but remains bottled up in the House.

In a moment of diplomatic excellence, "Butterbean" Esch, the prize fighter who was apparently never told that money was offered to his opponents to lose to him, told the investigator, "I didn't see anything at Top Rank that was criminal ... related to fighting."

Despite all of the evidence compiled by Big Frankie, Joey wonders why he's the only player from *Operation Matchbook* doing time. It sure doesn't seem like justice was served.

"[Senators Richard Bryan and John McCain] tried to do the right thing ... unfortunately, I think they faced on the federal level what I met on the state level," Oklahoma Labor Commissioner Reneau Wynn said. "There are too many people involved who would, basically, have to tell on themselves or admit that they're doing wrong."

A part of me wants to argue that the way Joey bamboozled the FBI—getting them to pay for his extravagent and expensive parties on an investigation that ultimately had few rewards—is about the punkest thing he could have done, given his situation, but ultimately it was his inside connections and charm that got the FBI inside Top Rank and the ineffectiveness of the investigation was unrelated to anything Joey had done.

So while it appears that Top Rank and the FBI may have bamboozled many people with relative impunity and there are times in his life that Joey may have been led on by empty promises while stuck between a rock and a hard place, it seems arguable that he has bamboozled his own fair share of people.

But forever only able to see his own suffering, Joey says, "I still can't understand why they're doing this to me."

Fiona Manning, a reporter for San Diego's *La Prensa*, shares the skeptical view of Joey's reform and expects Joey's pleading sob stories to continue. "You can bet, he'll let his fingers do the walking, looking for a new set of sympathetic ears."

And so in the end, who was bamboozled?

SUBSCRIBE TO EVERYTHING WE PUBLISH!

Do you love what Microcosm publishes?

Do you want us to publish more great stuff?

Would you like to receive each new title as it's published?

Subscribe as a BFF to our new titles and we'll mail them all to you as they are released!

$10-30/mo, pay what you can afford. Include your t-shirt size and month/date of birthday for a possible surprise! Subscription begins the month after it is purchased.

microcosmpublishing.com/bff